Praise for *Small Pleasures: Finding Grace in a Chaotic World*

This eloquent, profound, and moving book captures the spirit she has infused into New Dimensions Radio for more than three decades. Small Pleasures is a book of meditative essays that delivers on the promise of the title: they are a pleasure to read and will ease busy readers into a state of grace. . . . Read a meditation or two before going to sleep, and your dreams will herald a better tomorrow.
—Robert W. Fuller, former president of Oberlin College, author of *Somebodies and Nobodies* and *All Rise*

This is spiritual exploration that has been lived, stories culled from a wise and wild woman. Justine has mined the gold of her own experience and offers us practical wisdom and inspiration for living a full and deep life.
—Oriah Mountain Dreamer, author of *The Invitation*

This collection of essays by Justine Toms provides the reader a place not only for reflection, but inspiration and motivation for personal and social change. . . . A great book for opening to possibilities and re-dreaming one's life.
—Angeles Arrien, PhD, cultural anthropologist, author of *The Four-Fold Way* and *The Second Half of Life*

SMALL PLEASURES

FINDING GRACE IN A CHAOTIC WORLD

JUSTINE TOMS

HAMPTON ROADS
PUBLISHING COMPANY, INC.

Small Pleasures
Finding Grace in a Chaotic World

Justine Toms

Cover design by Gopa & Ted2, Inc.
Cover art by Getty Images

Hampton Roads Publishing Company, Inc.
1125 Stoney Ridge Road
Charlottesville, VA 22902
434-296-2772 • fax: 434-296-5096
e-mail: hrpc@hrpub.com • www.hrpub.com

If you are unable to order this book from your local
bookseller, you may order directly from the publisher.
Call 1-800-766-8009, toll-free.

Toms, Justine Willis.
  Small pleasures : finding grace in a chaotic world / Justine Toms.
      p. cm.
  Summary: "A collection of fifty short, meditative essays designed to
help people escape from their chaotic lives and focus instead on the little things that make life good, meaningful, and beautiful"--Provided by
publisher.
  ISBN-13: 978-1-57174-586-6 (5.25 x 7.25 tc : alk. paper)
  1. Peace of mind--Religious aspects. 2. Grace (Theology) I. Title.
  BL627.55.T66 2008
  204'.32--dc22
                                                    2008018790

ISBN 978-1-57174-586-6
10 9 8 7 6 5 4 3 2 1
Printed on acid-free paper in Canada

TABLE OF CONTENTS

FOREWORD

"Justine," I told her, "you had me at the subtitle!"

Had author Toms invited her readers to seek order in a chaotic world, or grace in a wicked one, I'd probably have had to read a bit farther in *Small Pleasures* (oh, maybe a page or two) before making my determination.

But the word *grace* brings one set of associations, and *chaotic* quite another—religious in the first, harking back at least as far as Saint Augustine, and scientific in the other. So by enclosing them in a single participial phrase, Justine hints at an intriguing possibility. Quietly understated as the short pieces are that comprise her book— "small pleasures" of the most accessible kind—might they also be read usefully in the context of an important public conversation that has turned of late into a loud and lamentably bitter row?

I think they might.

Because if I read *Small Pleasures* accurately, the grace that the author discovers as she struggles with one large, intractable question after another (and she is deeply attuned to the social and political realities of our time) is almost invariably hidden in plain sight, crying out for us to slow down, lift our gaze up, and *look* for it. Haven't the great Christian mystics told us over and over that the winds of grace are always blowing, that all we have to do is hoist our sails?

Just so, the proponents of complexity science tell us that when we think we see chaos—in weather, or economics, or human affairs—chances are very good that we're looking at order we're just not yet in a position to see. Our "chaotic world," they tell us, is only apparently so. Out of its very complexity—at the very edge of chaos—extraordinary new possibilities keep emerging.

Divine grace? Emergent qualities? Perhaps in a hundred years or so science and religion will have found their way to a *détente*—and to an altogether new way of talking about the mysterious phenomenon that presently dazzles both.

It's a curious thing, but true, I think, that when a woman writes a book the question *still* arises: "Is this a *woman's* book?" Because I hope that its readership includes men, and see no reason why it shouldn't, I would say, on one level, "absolutely not!"

But in fact it is one of the real strengths of *Small Pleasures* that it arises out of an implacably and unapologetically female sensibility, and, once again, emerging (!) science substantiates that observation.

What I have in mind is the fascinating discovery made about five years ago by a pair of UCLA scientists, who have shown that the "fight or flight" pattern that is supposed to characterize human beings' response to threat holds true for men, but not women. Think about our evolutionary history and we can see why. The most common threat to a woman probably wasn't the saber-toothed tiger or warrior from over the hill, but the man she shared a cave with—and in any case, neither fight nor flight is of much use if your children are close at hand. No, prehistoric women couldn't afford to be reactive—they had to be canny and resourceful. The children of the ones who were survived to have children of their own.

Women, it turns out, developed their own response to imminent crisis. Researchers Shelley Taylor and Laura Cousino Klein call it the "tend and befriend" response: in the face of incipient violence, you get very calm and very observant. You make sure everyone's fed and comfortable, you do what you can to defuse the tension in the room, and—this is the intriguing part—you form supportive reciprocal alliances with other females. Your sisters, your mother, your friends.

And of course all of this is orchestrated by the endocrinal system. The rush of adrenalin that sends testosterone levels sky-high in men prompts an oxytocin release in women. Oxytocin is the hormone that triggers the let-down response in nursing mothers, stimulates labor in birthing women, and encourages women to bond with other females. When a woman does connect with other women, she is rewarded with a release of dopamine, which activates the brain's "pleasure system."

The threats that women like Justine Toms and her friends are confronting today aren't domestic or even personal. They are global and almost inconceivably daunting. We *do* want to lash out, we *are* tempted to run away and hide. Yet over and over in these simple sketches, the perennial female wisdom of "tend and befriend" goes on declaring itself.

Wait. Slow down. Pay close attention. Feed anyone who's hungry, comfort anybody who's upset, fire up the oven. Call your best friend. . . .

Gently redirecting our attention away from the paralyzing crises of our time, Justine opens us out to the smallest of teachers—a spider no bigger than a freckle—and to the most unlikely—a goat named Sadie, or a baby Gray Whale off the coast of Baja. And when we've taken in what she has to tell us and we look back at the headlines afterward, our angle of vision has changed just a crucial little bit.

Justine reminds us how important it is to take care of the body, and she finds a hundred ways to remind us to slow down just when we think we should be kicking into high gear. She dazzles us by pointing out what we can observe when we do. She talks about hope and how it is sustained, and she conveys the riotous great fun that women can have together, especially when they are at their most serious.

One of the great delights of my writing life was being interviewed by Justine Toms: I've rarely felt as thoroughly *heard*. Much of the warmth and intelligence I encountered during that hour and a half shines through the pages of *Small Pleasures*.

—Carol Lee Flinders

Carol Lee Flinders lives at the Blue Mountain Center for Meditation in Northern California. She is the coauthor of *Laurel's Kitchen* and author of *Enduring Grace: Living Portraits of Seven Women Mystics, At the Root of This Longing, Rebalancing the World: Why Women Belong and Men Compete and How to Restore the Ancient Equilibrium,* and *Enduring Lives: Living Portraits of Women of Faith in Action.*

A WIDER LANDSCAPE:

How We See Ourselves and the World

A WIDER LANDSCAPE

R ev. Mary Manin Morrissey has said that anything in
the world we can see in full bloom started as a seed.
As I write this, we're entering the fourth decade since my
husband Michael and I founded New Dimensions Media
and Broadcasting Network. Looking back over those
years, I can see that the seed of that venture began in a
life-changing conversation he and I had when we first
met.

I grew up Episcopalian and loved my church, but in
my early twenties when I moved to Alabama I became a
Southern Baptist. I sang in the choir and taught Sunday
school and expressed my spiritual exuberance with my
new Baptist friends. In my late twenties I migrated to
California and became a Jehovah's Witness. Again, I
jumped in with both feet and was soon knocking on
doors spreading the "good news."

Then I met Michael. He, of course, was not a
Jehovah's Witness. Meeting him was like a thunderbolt.
I really wanted to get to know him better, but not before
we worked out what appeared to be a spiritual gulf
between us. I believed I was privy to "the Way, the Truth,
and the Light." He, in my eyes, was not. I phoned him

and said, "I'd like to come over and talk about spiritual matters." He agreed.

I walked into his townhouse with an armful of Jehovah's Witness translations of various spiritual texts, including the *New World* edition of the Bible. We went downstairs to his guest room, which he had turned into a library that was stacked from floor to ceiling with books. There were books about the Kabbalah, the I Ching, the Bhagavad Gita, Judaism, Vedanta, Science of Mind, and much more. Of course, I didn't want to talk about any of those works. I wanted only to talk about *my* religion using *my* translation of the Bible—and I told him so.

At that point Michael reached back on the shelf next to him and pulled out a green Bible and said, "You mean this one?"

The moment is ever vivid in my memory. As he pulled a copy of "my" Bible off his shelf I thought, "Maybe he's being more inclusive than I am." But I kept the notion to myself as we began the conversation. I'd entered his library with all my biases, prejudices, certainties, and enthusiasms firmly in place. I felt that my way was the "true" way. However, I could not help but notice that Michael had included "my way" in his own exploration, along with so many other great spiritual traditions. That aroused my curiosity.

Nevertheless, as we launched into our spiritual dialogue I remained staunchly in my own camp, representing my own interpretation of the truth. I would read a chapter and describe the historical context, then share the meaning that I felt was the "right" one, saying, "So you see this means such and such, it's quite obvious."

Michael would listen and respond with something like, "Yes, I see what you mean—and you might also look at it like this."

Every time he did that I became more and more excited, because rather than negating what I said, he enhanced it. He took my view and couched it in a more spacious landscape. The boundaries of my spiritual ideals were being broadened and extended. If he had said, "No, you are wrong. It is this way," I most likely would have resisted, and in all probability there would not be a New Dimensions today.

Michael and I stayed up the entire night talking about spiritual matters. Nine months later we started our business. I realize now that, mythologically speaking, we conceived New Dimensions in those quiet hours before dawn more than thirty-five years ago. That conversation continues, only now we have microphones and guests, and hundreds of thousands of listeners are included in the conversation.

Try not to doubt the power of your own curiosity and inquiry. Mine has been the guiding force behind the wondrous journey that has defined my life. In hindsight I know that in those years of shifting from one church to another after another, it wasn't about dogma and it wasn't about settling down and no longer asking the questions about why we are here and what our purpose is. What I was searching for all along was the biggest spiritual truth I could find. In fact, I continue to inquire, probe, and puzzle for a broad landscape of wisdom and meaning. I've found some answers, and I know there are more to come.

What have you hung your hat on that forms the foundation of your spiritual faith? What are you still curious and uncertain about? What has stood the test of your experience and scrutiny? Have you staked out your territory and set up your tent on the side of the mountain, or are you willing to continue up to the summit and see what is on the other side?

If you've chosen to set your sights on the summit, you'll find the horizons are wider than you can imagine. And there's always another mountain to climb, another summit to attain, and each new landscape is more vast than the one you left behind.

WHAT'S IT ALL ABOUT?

Recently I gave myself the gift of a detox retreat at the Optimum Health Institute in San Diego, California. This is a place where you can give your digestive process a break using a cleansing diet along with freshly juiced wheat grass. During my stay, there were about a hundred participants, and, as you can imagine, some significant conversations unfolded as we took our minds off our stomachs and started exercising other aspects of being.

On one occasion I sat on the lawn with the soft winter sun gently warming me and had a pleasant exchange with Len Wechsler, a tall, lean man whose deep brown eyes and impish smile told me that the little boy was alive and well within. A spontaneous storytelling moment emerged as we challenged one another to share interesting stories about our lives.

Len offered a memory of Harvey Goldberg, a gifted professor he had the privilege of meeting during his undergraduate studies at the University of Wisconsin in Madison. Len's eyes welled up with tears as if forty years had not passed since he was enrolled in Professor Goldberg's class, "The History of Contemporary Revolutions," which examined twentieth-century uprisings

7

in Iran, Poland, Japan, France, and many other countries. My friend told of how his teacher stood at the lectern each day and taught without the aid of notes. That semester the course was so popular that it was moved three times to ever larger lecture halls—and still the class had standing room only.

Len described for me the final lecture of the course. "Goldberg taught up to the last minute of the last day, teaching right up to the bell. He says, 'Well, we are done.' He turned his back to the students as if to close the class. Then, turning back toward the shining young faces, he said, 'You want me to tell you what it is all about? You want to know? I'm going to tell you.' All of us are on the edge of our seats, holding our breath, knowing that in a moment the secret of it all would be revealed. He says, 'Everything we've done this semester, the courses you have taken are good, but none of that matters.' He waits, and it feels like he looks each one of us in the eyes. Then the old man says, 'Love—that's what it is all about.' With that he left the room. Everyone was crying."

Professor Goldberg was right. Love is the way in and love is the way out. Love is the path, the process, the key.

May your life be filled with love.

SMALL PLEASURES

My husband, Michael, gifted me with the book *My Name Escapes Me* by Sir Alec Guinness. Michael said he thought I'd like it. He knows me well. I couldn't put the book down. It's a log of Sir Alec's weekly activities over several years. He was a superb actor, a master of disguise, admired worldwide, knighted by Queen Elizabeth, and the recipient of awards galore. One might imagine his days filled with the excitement of living in the fast lane, wining and dining with other famous people. But there was a sweetness about Sir Alec's day-to-day living that completely captivated me. His days were filled less with life in the fast lane than with visits to his fishpond and trips to the local nursery in the fall for bulbs for his spring blooms. He attended and hosted intimate dinner parties. He'd get a new pair of glasses in London, and complain about the noise of the freeway traffic on the M-5. He took great pleasure in wandering through various art galleries and delighted in sitting in the warm sun with friends.

As iconic as Sir Alec Guinness appears from a distance, the things he found worth writing about were the simple things. And in truth, his daily routine was not unlike my own and most probably was similar to yours as well. Our lives are made up of small pleasures—I'm sure your day looks a lot like mine. A poignant email about a cowboy arrives and I pass it on to friends. I say hello to the woman at the checkout stand at the local grocery, and we chat about our respective busy days. I no longer have to give my name at the cleaners because I'm welcomed like an old friend as soon as I walk in the door. It makes me smile. When I get home, I pause at the front door to admire the way the mist glows in the full moon. I say hello to my cat, speaking as if she understands every word—and she does. She talks back in cat language, and I understand her as well. It is no small miracle. A new Congress is installed, and my cymbidiums are blooming.

As I write this I can hear Michael laughing in the other room while he talks on the phone. I take a break from my computer screen to look out the window of my office and admire the Mayacamas mountain range reflecting rosy hues in the setting sun. The resident pigeons do their calisthenics, flying around in circles as they do each day about this time for no apparent reason other than the joy of it.

It's late in winter now, and I feel quiet in this time before the yellow flowers start to bud in the vineyards or the electrifying green of new leaves appears on the trees. I'm grateful that this new year has begun slowly . . . spaciously. It has given me time to reflect on the small pleasures that make up my life, and I vow to do my best to be more fully present to them in the year to come. After all, they are the fabric of life, the substance that is ever present between the peaks and valleys.

HANGING OUT IN THE LANDSCAPE OF DIFFICULTIES

Some years ago I was serving on the board of directors of a nonprofit organization that was going through difficulties. I remember one particular board meeting when the twelve of us were working with great concentration to come up with some steps to recommend to the executive committee. It was heavy going, and I felt uncomfortable as the discussion remained stuck in the throes of the dilemma.

I felt an intense inner pressure to find a solution. So I chirped brightly, "I know what we should do. Let's break up into three groups and each come up with an answer, then come back together and compare our answers to decide which is the best one."

I was proud of myself. My theory, to divide us up in order to conquer the difficulty, seemed like such a reasonable approach. I was sure it would help us move quickly to the more enjoyable activity of mapping out solutions.

However, I was overruled when a fellow board member made a statement that forever changed my view of creative problem solving. He said, "Justine, I appreciate your suggestion, but I'm not ready to work on solutions. I need to hang out in the landscape of the difficulty a while before I feel I can start finding answers."

His comments helped me realize that I had a low tolerance for hanging out with problems. My tendency was to want to move quickly to solutions. But it soon became clear why that would not serve the overall health of the organization. As our group spent time that evening exploring the dynamics of the difficulties the organization faced, I began to realize that creative solutions are very deeply connected to the dynamics that created the trouble in the first place. By understanding the pathway that led to the knotted strands that had a stranglehold on what was not working, a plethora of possibilities revealed themselves.

No doubt we all have circumstances in our lives that are difficult, bound up by invisible knots of complicated energy. Through the years I've come to understand that staying with a challenge until it is fully understood is the key. In fact, I now find it exciting to loosen the snarled strands that hold a tricky situation together. It's a little like unraveling a mass of tangled string. By unraveling the knots of energy and staying in the landscape of concern with curiosity and detached awareness, one has a better chance of finding creative solutions.

ALL YOU NEED IS LOVE

When Michael and I were giving a workshop on "Deep Listening in Changing Times," I found myself talking about love. I've thought a lot about love and tried to pin it down, to dissect it so that I can help myself and others understand how to find it and keep it. But love has been elusive—not love itself, but its definition. It doesn't want to be framed and hung on the wall; it wants to be flowing and moving.

One afternoon during the workshop I surprised myself when I responded to a question from one of the participants. "Love is a congruence, an unimpeded flow of energy between two people. Love tends to awaken connection rather than separation." Love attracts; it is the glue of the cosmos. Planets *love* their star. Star clusters *love* their galaxies. Bees *love* their flowers. Flowers *love* their bees.

This metaphor holds up when there is a natural affinity between two people. However, you might ask, "What if there is a person in my life whom I just can't love? There is someone who presses my hot buttons, acts like sandpaper to my soul. How can I love and honor this person? How can I connect? How can I be less afraid of our interactions?"

Each of us has had someone like this in our lives at one time or another. A guided meditation given by the Unity minister Joan Gattuso has been very helpful to me in dealing with these challenging relationships. She helps us visualize those scary persons in our lives and see them at different stages in their lives, all the way back to when they were infants, with bright, innocent eyes looking out at the world. Joan reminds us that we can ignore the light in others or we can deny it, but we cannot totally obscure their light or ours. There is an innocent and lovable person inside each of us. If we focus on this, the lovable parts will expand and grow in our relationships. Joan describes it this way: "When we come from a place of looking for the lovely, then we experience miracles and life opens for us. Love attracts love."

When I am in the presence of those who appear to be unlovely, I try to remember to take a deep breath, look into their eyes, and silently beam loving thoughts to them. I know that when I extend love I will always receive love,

LET YOUR LIGHT SHINE

and I'll remain connected to the light in others just as the planets are eternally connected to their stars.

LET YOUR LIGHT SHINE

Have you ever awakened in the middle of the night feeling plagued by fears and worries, so much so that it is hard to get back to sleep? If so, you're not alone. There are many nights I'm probably awake the same time you are, fretting away until the wee hours.

It's reasonable to assume that those nighttime panics emerge from negative thoughts and fears we harbor through the day. Recently I began to ask myself, "Just how much time *do* I spend each day in a negative field of consciousness?" If it is true our thoughts are like magnets, and good ones attract positive energy and bad ones attract the negative stuff, then how do we balance that out?

I must admit that, when I realistically take an inventory of my daily thoughts, I find the fearful thoughts often outweigh the loving ones. So how do I ever get ahead? For example, if I can spend ten minutes each day luxuriating in the awareness that the universe is abundant and really supports me, what about the other twenty-three hours and fifty minutes when I'm neutral, anxious, or worried? Okay, so add an hour of meditation, an hour of swimming, plus sleep—I'm still left with plenty of time to feel bombarded by news and information about terrorism, my own personal health, the health of my loved ones, money, *E. coli* bacteria in spinach, global warming, and all the rest. How *will* I ever balance the negative energy with the positive?

Not long ago a dear friend and I were talking about the seemingly universal human phenomenon of those sleepless, fretful nights, and how the panic and distress can overtake us. We fantasized about how great it would be to solve the problem once and for all, to make it go away, never to return. However, the solution seemed to be more akin to doing the dishes or dusting the bookshelves, things that need to be done on a regular basis. There is no final victory; only vigilance over the quality of our thoughts will be effective against this underlying anxiousness that invades our sleep, and our waking states as well.

But banishing the negativity may not be as hard as you'd think. In my talk with my friend, she reminded me that all the great teachers and avatars say that positive thought is infinitely greater and more powerful than negative thought; therefore, it doesn't need to occupy an equal amount of time. To make a long story short, one can think more negative than positive thoughts and still come out ahead.

Recently I've had some help in turning my anxieties into creative possibilities. At least once a year I have a psychic checkup, and at my last visit my psychic doctor gave me a wonderful game to play when I get into those negative loops. It's called the "Wouldn't It Be Wonderful?" game, and it goes like this: When you find yourself feeling stuck, looping around and around a problem, you ask yourself, "Wouldn't it be wonderful if . . . ?" Then play around with some fabulous, even outlandish scenarios. For example, *wouldn't it be wonderful if* someone called me out of the blue and said, "I've loved the *New Dimensions* program for years and years, and would really like to give an endowment"? I ask myself that question, then indulge in thinking about all the good things that would come out of something like that. I'm smiling right now, as I let all the positive benefits of my solution roll over me. Or *wouldn't it be wonderful if* Jews, Muslims, and Christians in the Middle East all laid down their weapons and began to live in peace with one another? Wow, my imagination really goes wild with that possibility!

When you play this game you'll notice it not only benefits your mind, but your whole body starts to relax as you engage all kinds of fun and amazing possibilities. It is especially good for your adrenal glands, which produce three major classes of hormones that are essential for your day-to-day ability to handle stress.

While I'm not a doctor, I do know that the medical field is coming to a better understanding of the body-mind-spirit connection. When you bring positive energy into your field of being, it attracts more positive energy. When you're in a dark, negative place, you're like a light-house with the light turned off. But when you switch on the light, all sorts of rescue boats that are out there (like good hormones) looking for your new bright signal will come rushing in to help.

So next time you up wake in the middle of the night with anxieties and worries, remember to turn on your light by asking yourself, *Wouldn't it be wonderful if . . . ?*

THE HABITS OF YOUR MIND

I was struck by the words of Tulku Thondup Rinpoche in a recent *New Dimensions* interview. He said that the only thing we take with us when we die are our habits of mind. I've heard this before—in fact, I've been hearing it from various masters for more than thirty years. Yet this time the words had a visceral impact on my mind and body. I don't know why. Maybe it's because I'm getting older and feeling my mortality in more immediate terms. Maybe it's because I've recently been thinking a lot about the concepts of forgiveness and of sympathetic joy, and how far short of these feelings I so often fall.

When Rinpoche spoke about the habits of mind I could feel the immediacy of the call, a sense that there is no time to waste because I cannot know when the moment of my death will arrive. Oh, I know I "should" change my habits simply because my life would be better. But somehow I felt more motivated to really do it when I heard him speak of the time when there is no longer anything we can do to alter our lives for the better. It would be great if we could show up in our afterlives saying, "Oh, I didn't have time to really practice new habits. I intended to. Can't I just slip this habit off and enter my new life after life with a clean slate?" Yeah, right. As they say, that and $2.50 will get you a good cup of coffee.

The idea of changing an ingrained habit is truly daunting. I've failed so many times. I really do want to change the litany of doubt, regret, mean feelings, worry, fear, and distress. So I asked myself some hard questions. How can I change my negative thoughts into loving, life-enhancing ones? What is the opposite of fear? Is it love? The emotions of love and fear are so basic and so huge; it's hard for me to come up with concrete ways to turn fear into love. So I've decided to start with some other malady. Maybe I'll have an easier time with worry.

I can easily get my brain around worry. I know what it feels like; I know its content well. I took a moment to look at what may be across the continuum from worry. I decided that for me it is gratitude. What if instead of whirling my mind around with worry, I'm dancing with gratitude?

Okay, great. How do I start to make a new practice in my life? Here's what I've come up with. First, I need to become aware of the moments when I'm in my worry mode, those times when my brain is spinning out its tale of how bad things are, and how they have always been bad, and how they will most likely continue to be bad. As soon as I'm conscious that I'm running the worry channel, I switch it—just like clicking a TV remote—to the gratitude channel, and ask myself what I am grateful for in that moment. I change my focus.

For example, I often find myself operating in that negative mode when I'm in the car. As soon as I realize I'm spinning out my worry list, I look around at the landscape as if waking from a dream. It's a trick of the mind— it's immediate. I switch my channel and am grateful for the miracle that other drivers are paying attention and we're able to rip down the road at sixty-five miles an hour and not run into one another.

My prayer each morning is to become more and more aware of my habitual negative thought patterns, then practice more and more to change them. As you know, we can be in a worry mode and not be aware of it. I have no idea what percentage of the time I'm spinning negative thoughts or positive ones. But I pray that each day I become ever more aware of my life-destructive habits of thinking, and replace them with life-enhancing ones.

Try this simple technique for yourself: When you find yourself thinking negative thoughts, just change the channel. Does it help? Are you more relaxed? Are you happier? When is it most difficult? If you can remember to turn a life-negating thought to a life-supporting one at least once a day, you are on your way to changing the habit. Merely noticing that you are in a gloomy state is a big step in the right direction.

ANGER HAS NO ARMS OR LEGS

Early this morning I was contemplating the Buddhist saying, "Anger has no arms or legs," when an old episode of *Star Trek* came to mind. It's been a long time since I've seen it, so pardon me if some of the details are a little off. The gist of the story and the core lesson, though, remain clear.

There is an invisible entity that has entered the *Enterprise*. The crew can't see it, but the audience can. It appears as a swirling energy pattern near the ceiling and moves about the ship at will. Klingons are on the ship fighting one-on-one with members of the Federation crew. Every time there is a fight, the swirling energy pattern gets bigger. We, the audience, can see that this entity gets its energy from anger, fighting, and negativity in general. At some point, Captain Kirk and his crew figure this out and negotiate with the Klingons to be friendly. An extraordinary scene unfolds: These mortal enemies begin to walk about the ship with their arms around one another in joyous camaraderie. They laugh and joke and poke fun at one another with good humor. As they do, the malevolent presence begins to dwindle until it is just a wisp, and it finally leaves the ship for lack of the energy on which it depends for its survival.

This *Star Trek* episode helps me visualize what takes place when I feed my anger, frustration, and bitterness. I give my anger arms and legs, so to speak. I help it to get around. I give it a form that it otherwise does not have. It is a parasite that hitches a ride with me; it travels with me as long as I feed it and carry it.

Just yesterday I got really angry in response to a dear and longtime friend's negative comments. I felt justified as I escalated the negativity with my own angry words. In truth, I came out with my guns blazing in reaction.

Now, in a more centered, calm place, without self-recrimination, I contemplate yesterday's anger. I can't change the past, but I can take time out to look at how anger is or is not effective. What was it I wanted in that situation? Did I get what I wanted? Was there a more effective action I could have chosen? If so, what was it?

There are, most likely, many courses of action I could have taken. I didn't feel motivated to go directly into laughter and camaraderie, as the Federation crew did with the Klingons. But instead of reacting in anger, I could have immediately and quietly removed myself from the situation. Leaving the scene would have accomplished two things. It would have taken me away from the irritant, and it would have made it clear to my friend that I would not stand in the field of that kind of negative energy, that I would not tolerate being talked to in such a manner. Leaving would have been kinder, both to me and to her, and would have created a space for my friend and me to move more quickly back to love.

At the root of all of our longings and our greatest desires is the wish to love and be loved. My own angry words, and no doubt the negative comments of my friend, were ultimately rooted in that desire. My reaction gave arms and legs to anger, and made fulfilling the desire for love more difficult. Walking away would have made it easier.

I realize we can't change our past angers, but I suggest that we contemplate the choices we can make. Rather than giving anger a ride, let us give our arms and legs to love.

ARE YOU A "SPARKLE BRAIN"?

Events that occur in threes tend to get my attention. In the past few days I've had dynamic conversations with three different people who are well into their eighties, and our discussions centered on a variety of interests and activities. One was taking a course at the local college to learn how to use the computer his family had given him. Another was a retired forester who now keeps himself busy as a gardener. The third person was ordering a tape of a program he had heard on *New Dimensions*, an interview with physicist Peter Russell about science and spirit. What made the conversations feel so similar was the twinkle, the spark, the sense of aliveness that radiated from each of these elders. All three were a delight. We laughed and joked with one another and talked about our common dreams.

These three "sparkle brain" people reminded me of a magazine article I read some years ago. I can no longer recall what magazine it was, but I distinctly remember the survey it reported because it validated my own experience. The study investigated characteristics of people who live to be over a hundred and remain vital, healthy, and energized. Researchers found four habits in common among the centenarians they surveyed. They're habits that all of us might want to cultivate.

1. Continue to learn new things. This keeps the mind supple. It activates the neurons in the brain. Just as we need to move our joints to keep them lubricated, so the brain needs the lubrication of learning. It could be something as simple as memorizing a new poem or as complex as learning a new language. It could mean taking up knitting or bird watching. It doesn't seem to matter what the activity is, so long as it involves learning.

2. Do something meaningful so that you know and feel you're making a contribution to others. This prevents us from getting too immersed in ourselves and our own problems, aches, and pains. It seems to be programmed into human DNA to want to contribute to the lives of others. We are, after all, a tribal species. We feel good when we serve others. Send a card to someone who is sick, or pray for that person. Serve at a local food bank or thrift shop or read to the elderly. There are as many ways to serve others as there are people. Each week my eighty-seven-year-old aunt goes to the home for seniors and reads to the elderly. She also participates in a theater group and continues to edit, copyright, and send off her plays to her agent. Those who participate feel better about themselves, and this naturally leads to a more energized body and mind.

3. Stay flexible; don't feel you need to be in control. We are not in control anyway. The only thing we truly control is our response to what happens to us. The battle that arises inside and around us when we constantly need to be in control of people and events exhausts the mind, body, and spirit. Rolling with the punches and seeing the opportunities in life's challenges leads to a healthier perspective and helps us to be more physically healthy as well.

4. Develop the ability to adapt to loss. This is especially important as we age. Grief occurs when we lose loved ones and dear friends. Difficult as it is, it is necessary to feel that grief if we are to remain vital. It is also important not to wallow in it, which inhibits our capacity to allow new friends into our lives.

The three "sparkle brain" elders I spoke with possessed all of these qualities. They helped me remember that these attributes are not just for centenarians, like those in the study, but also for my friends in their eighties, their sixties, or their forties—they're important for all of us. We need to practice them in the present and receive the benefits in the present, no matter our age. As the Tibetan lama and teacher Sogyal Rinpoche says, "If you want to know your past life, look into your present condition. If you want to know your future life, look into your present actions."

THE OTHER

SIDE OF THE STORY

I don't know about you, but I've been feeling quite a bit of stress lately. I think it is a combination of the times, information overload, and letting myself get caught up in the conflicts and struggles of the world at large—and in my small corner of it. In response to my prayer for help, I ran across some writing I did a while ago on the martial art of aikido.

Aikido, as you may know, is not founded on the principle of winning or losing, or even seeking a stalemate. Instead, the practice has two main objectives. The first is to move in and face the world as your opponent faces the world, that is, to truly see as clearly as you can from that person's perspective without losing your own. The second tenet is to try to do no harm, to actually protect the attacker by using a minimum of force and maintaining a grounded and centered perspective. In theory it sounds rather easy, but we all know this is a philosophy that takes a lifetime of practice and asks of us a depth of understanding that can challenge us for that long as well.

Several years ago Michael and I and three of our colleagues felt this philosophy guiding us while we were in Mexico doing interviews about the threatened migration patterns of the monarch butterfly. The situation is complex and intertwined with poverty, ecology, education, tradition, oppression, history, governance, multinational issues, human foibles, and on and on and on. Over and over we found our quick-fix ideas falling apart in the short time it took us to discuss them. Deep listening seemed to be the order of the day as we were required to sink our rods of understanding further into the history and reality of the culture of Mexico to comprehend more fully the scope of the problem. Thus, we were invited first to turn and face the world as a *compasino*, or farm worker, does, then to see it through the eyes of a government official, and yet again to look at it from the perspective of a biologist.

Practicing this art of seeing through the eyes of another and doing no harm seems to be about the best advice I've heard in a long time. It reminds me to stop and breathe, and gives me a mantra to say silently to myself as I feel my blood boiling about one current issue or another. Take a breath, "See it as the other sees it; I will do no harm," release breath. Take a breath, "See it as the other sees it; I will do no harm," release breath. Take another breath, "See it as the other sees it; I will do no harm," release breath. Ah.

Here is a practice you might try. Close your eyes and feel an issue in your life that is upsetting to you, something that brings up strong feelings of frustration. It can be something close to you, in your household or your workplace, or it can be a conflict on a more global scale. Now imagine yourself in the place of each of the characters involved. If the situation involves several people with a variety of viewpoints, place yourself in the position of caring for each of them and respecting their viewpoints one at a time. Let go of your judgments of right or wrong, and allow yourself to feel through that individual's eyes.

If the issue involves several groups of people with different perspectives, choose one person who represents each group, and stand in that person's shoes, see the situation through that person's eyes, and feel your heart care about that person's experience of things.

Do this exercise with each person or group involved in the conflict until you are able to see the issue from each of the different perspectives. Now write in your journal about the insights you've gained from standing in the others' shoes.

 ## A Sense of Place

I magine yourself in the Deep South, opening a wrought-iron gate at the bottom of an azalea-bordered, oak-lined hill. You walk down a sidewalk and climb several flights of steps as you approach a Victorian house as lovely as a wedding cake. Note the tower that dominates the left front corner as you ascend the wide staircase that leads to a generous, wraparound porch.

Around back there is an ancient pear tree sporting a crutch to hold up a heavy limb, overburdened by ripening fruit, that extends over the walkway. Gracing the side yard is a lily pond with frogs making monster sounds that are much too big for their small bodies. Under your feet you feel the reverberation of a steam locomotive on the rail behind the houses across the street, struggling to get traction as it begins to move out of town. Steam rises off the pavement in the aftermath of the window-rattling, thunderous downpour that just roared through the blistering hot August afternoon.

This is my ancestral home in east-central Alabama, built by my great-grandfather, Reuben Herzfeld, in the 1890s.

Whenever I think of this enchanted place, a sense of sweetness sweeps over me. It is the abode of nearly all my childhood summers, Christmases, and Easters. It is here that I rode my first horse, Buttermilk, round and round the front yard. I played dress-up in the spacious bedrooms and spent warm summer afternoons rolling down the hill with my three siblings and our eight cousins. My mother and her three sisters were born in this house. My grandparents and their parents died here. It continues to speak to me in my dreams. I feel safe in this place, whether I arrive in person or visit in my imagination or my dreams. The house, the land, the very air of it envelops me with generous hospitality and warmth.

William Poy Lee, first-generation Chinese American author of *The Eighth Promise: An American Son's Tribute to His Toisanese Mother,* tells of visiting his ancestral roots in the Pearl River Valley of southeastern China. He says, "Suddenly I started to bubble and started to feel this happiness and joy and hilarity. I literally could not stop chuckling for two or three days." He goes on to observe, "What I realized when I looked back on this was that I had come back to a place where we had lived for a thousand years. That particular soil and my body physically are very, very similar. I can't get away from that. What I felt was that I had gone to the tuning fork of my body, my spirit, and my being. That is why I was reaching my perfect pitch as a sentient being on this planet. This led me to wonder what the price of our constant mobility really is."

I feel fortunate that I have a similar sense of a place that's my "tuning fork," even though mine has not been inhabited for thousands of years by my ancestors—just a hundred or so.

The magical house of my childhood memories was spacious and included seven bedrooms. Grandmother employed a full-time cook and a part-time housekeeper, so her daughters felt no compunction in dropping off their children to spend their summers as a tribe in that small southern town. I loved being part of the tribe. There were nine pairs of roller skates for the older children, and we made good use of them, traveling in frenzied circles around the house.

Best of all was what we called the "dress-up" room. In the back bedroom of the second floor there was a huge cedar walk-in closet where Grandmother stored all the old clothes. She kept everything: Halloween costumes, discarded dresses our mothers and aunts had left behind, old military uniforms their husbands had worn, and the pièce de résistance—The Wedding Dress.

The six of us granddaughters were especially attracted to the white satin and lace gown. It was a fairy-tale dress, with a ruffle that draped just off the shoulders and sleeves that tapered snugly all the way down to the wrists. True to its era, it had a long train that elegantly flowed from the hem. But it was the veil that made us all catch our breath. It was made of tulle attached to a crown of white flowers. Juliette, my sister and the oldest cousin, had the honor of carefully unwrapping it from its delicate tissue paper, then each of us reverently took a turn trying it on.

There were scary places, too, in Grandmother's house. To avoid being snatched away by who-knows-what, we had to hurry past the big closet nestled under the front staircase at the far end of the foyer. This central greeting hall was so large that the light didn't penetrate its back recesses, and with the overhanging staircase it was tailor-made for goblins and ghosts to pop out if we weren't paying attention. The same was true of the narrow stairs that led to the attic. In order to get to the dress-up room we had to pass that creepy staircase and often heard ghostly sounds exhaling from it.

On any late summer afternoon, Papa, as we called our grandfather, could be found on the side porch, swinging in a hammock with several of us snuggled beside him. As the rotating fan turned slowly overhead, he sang Stephen Foster songs and spirituals. "Camptown ladies sing this song, doo-dah, doo-dah. . . . Swing low, sweet chariot."

Miss Roxie Miller was the cook. She was a large African American woman of undetermined age, not young, not old. She purposely tore holes in the tops and sides of her shoes. "It's so my feet can breathe," she told us. Miss Roxie was also a healer who could communicate directly with the animals. There were two cats in the house. One was an orange tabby we called Spencer, the other a gray tabby named Dinky. When Spencer got hit by a car, Dinky came to the kitchen door and made all sorts of sounds. Some of them were definite meows, others were half growls mixed with purrs. Miss Roxie listened carefully. Taking off her apron, she shoved open the screen door and rushed down the steps. We all followed close behind down the back walk to where Spencer lay on the side of the road. His injuries were extensive, and he soon died. We were all very sad. But to this day it amazes me that Miss Roxie could understand cat language. How did she know that Dinky was asking her to follow him?

Miss Roxie laughed a lot, and I'm convinced it was part of her healing art. Her laughter was so robust that we could hear it ring out throughout the entire house. And how she could cook! Sometimes she'd let us roll dough with her and make miniature biscuits.

My brothers and I would fight over who would have the special privilege of ringing the bell to call everyone to mealtime. On Sundays we often had fried chicken. One day my brother Jeff challenged us to witness the killing of the chicken. We were all too proud to say no. Solemnly we accompanied Miss Roxie to the chicken yard and watched her fearlessly grab a hen and take her out of the pen. We marched behind Miss Roxie to the back of the garage where, with a deft flick of her wrist, she separated the hen's body from her head. We were transfixed as we watched the headless chicken flap around, dancing until she exhausted herself and keeled over dead. How did she do that?

When I finally married and had a home of my own to look after, I thanked Grandmother for all those wonderful meals that she and Miss Roxie had put on the table for us. She'd smile coyly, and say, "Oh honey, it was nothing." She then told me about her secret strategy. She revealed that she always made sure the first meal we enjoyed upon arriving had all the fixings of a grand holiday meal. The last meal before we left was the same. Grandmother explained that she knew those were the only meals we would remember, and confided that the ones in between were more or less plain and simple affairs. Well, maybe so. But, honestly, I can not remember a single "plain" meal ever served up in that house.

Grandmother's father lived in the big house as well. He was a gaunt man who used a cane. Once a week, without fail, he'd walk with his slow but determined gait into town to get his beard trimmed. He was a man of few words and most of the time his weathered face carried a rather stern expression. He lived into his early nineties, and we were all a little scared of him. He looked like the picture of Jesus that hung over his bed, and had a little palsy in his hands. At dinnertime we stared at him with rapt attention as he scooped up a line of peas onto his knife. How did he get them in his mouth without spilling them? We tried to imitate this feat when he wasn't watching, but even with our steady, youthful coordination we never came close to matching his success.

As you can imagine, keeping up such a palatial estate could sorely tax any budget; our family finally, and reluctantly, sold it in 1993. But we were fortunate to find buyers who were able to bring it back to its youthful glory. They installed full bathrooms in each of the upstairs bedrooms, restored the gardens, and upgraded the kitchen and the wiring. It is now the Mistletoe Bough Bed & Breakfast. It even appeared one year on the cover of the *National Directory of Bed & Breakfast Inns in America*. You can see a picture of it online at www.mistletoebough.com. If you find yourself in Alexander City, Alabama, check it out. Or make it a destination!

These memories create a tapestry that gives me a sense of place. I believe it continues to influence my character in some deep and fundamental way. Most of us have our own story of a special childhood place that lives on in our hearts. Whether or not we ever get to revisit it in body, it is always available in spirit. This place helps form the ground of our being and is the root of our root, forever linking us to the passions, excitement, and discoveries of childhood. We can return to it as a positive touchstone as we step into the future.

ANIMALS AND NATURE

AS TEACHERS

NATURE RENEWS THE SPIRIT

E ach year Michael and I try to take a few days for rest and recuperation at Yosemite National Park. In this changing world, we find it refreshing to experience the timeless nature of Yosemite. It is as grand as ever. El Capitan, the awesome granite rock face, continues in its watchful stillness, guarding the entrance to the valley. Half-Dome perseveres across the ages as it reflects the full moon. Happy Isles gurgles and burbles as much as ever. Serenity prevails . . . no cares, no hustle-bustle, no computers, very few cars. Even the bears amble through the seasons as they've done for centuries. All is well in this pristine natural cathedral.

Taking time out to be in nature never fails to refresh and renew me on some deep level. It helps to slow me down and gives me a moment to pause and be ever grateful for my life, my friends, and my work.

Is there a place you love, a spot that never fails to renew your spirit as Yosemite does for me? Did you just sigh a deep sigh, or is there a smile on your face as you think of it? If so, when was the last time you went there for a visit? Is it time to schedule a weekend, a week, or a month in a place that nurtures your soul?

OF CREEKS AND SPIDERS

While thumbing through an old issue of *National Geographic*, I came across a fascinating article entitled "Deadly Silk: The Spider's Web" by Richard Conniff. I was captivated by his description of a spider of the genus *Wendilgarda*. This remarkable spider is no bigger than a freckle, but she has skills I'd like to emulate. Here is Conniff's description: "[She] strings a sort of tightrope across a stream and 'glues' her web to running water . . . thirteen separate [web] lines down to the surface, like the leaders on a fisherman's trotline. The riffle of the stream kept the end of each line skating back and forth in search of water striders." This tiny creature attaches her silk thread to *running* water. Conniff comments that this is "something humans cannot achieve with our best super-glues."

I am amazed by the image of this minute creature gluing herself to the relentless movement of the flowing stream. How does she calculate the faithful degree of flexibility to stay connected, anchored, yet not be washed away or drowned by the stream's ceaseless current?

It's almost as though *Wendilgarda* uses her web line to ground herself in the creek, much as we strive to ground ourselves when we need stability in our lives. We see our-selves growing imaginary roots into the earth to keep ourselves calm, centered, and stable in the face of life's challenges. This image makes sense; after all, we want to stand on firm ground and stay rooted in our truths, beliefs, and values. It feels comfortable, reliable, predica-ble. To be attached to water suggests being rootless, ungrounded, even dangerous. Yet this little spider thrives on it; her very life depends on it.

I wonder at the correlation between this tiny arach-nid's life and my own. How can I embrace the ceaseless flow of doings, commitments, engagements, and general undertakings—the streams of my life—without being washed away by its strong currents? How may I stay "webbed" in the fullness of life as a flowing stream?

To imagine ourselves being rooted to the earth like a great tree can help us to feel stable, steadfast, fixed in certainty about the past, our history, home, ancestry, job, religion, and community. However, the energy currents of the twenty-first century—the flowing stream of the electronic age—constantly present myriad options and opportunities. They are all but irresistible. This, now this, then this floats by for our nourishment and our innate creativity. Being grounded, connected to our roots, gives us faith in our ethics, values, moral code, our very integrity. But can we stand on terra firma at all times, or does life require us to dance with the elements, to skate over the currents?

How can we hold both the image of the tree and that of the spider? Can we draw upon our roots, all that we hold dear from our past, *and* be like the spider who, through her connection with the stream, leads us into the future, feeding our creativity and inspiring the dance of our lives?

I believe we must do both. We must root ourselves in the positive values and ethics that reflect the best of who we are as a species—*and* we must glue our web lines to the ever-moving stream of the present moment and dance with the extraordinary possibilities that float by.

DREAMS OF HORSES

"Anyone who has admired a horse galloping across a field has stepped into his or her mythic life, if only for a moment. These individuals have had a taste of the intimate relationship between horses and humans that has spanned centuries and populated one great story after another, entertaining, teaching, and inspiring us. Because of this rich heritage that has bound our lives to theirs, by their very nature, horses are mythic creatures.

They have become associated in our collective imagination with aspects of the human journey at its greatest."
  —Patricia Broersma, *Riding into Your Mythic Life*

My best girlfriend in grade school, Annie Palenske, had a horse. I didn't give this fact much thought at first, because my life was full of dogs, cats, and parakeets. I'd also enjoyed the company of a few small turtles, until my attention wavered. By the time I thought of them again they had become fossilized shadows of the green active playthings Daddy had brought home. But once I was introduced to the world of horses I was completely smitten and vowed I'd be the most responsible caregiver the world has known, if only I could have a horse of my own.

It all started innocently enough when I was nine years old, and Annie asked me if I'd like to come to the stable with her after school. Little did I know that I was about to fall completely and irretrievably in love with horses. It wasn't a gradual awakening of affection. It was a thunderbolt. Clearly, the horse goddess Epona had known long before I did that I belong to the tribe She Who Loves Horses. With her magical powers Epona switched on the dormant gene that lay dark and deep in my DNA. One moment I'd never given horses a passing thought, and in the time it takes to say *abracadabra* they became the center of my life.

On that fateful afternoon, Annie began by introducing me to her horse. He was a grand palomino named, of course, Trigger. First we entered his stall and I helped her brush his golden coat. Then she asked me to bring the saddle to her. I tried to lift it, but it was so heavy and unfamiliar in my hands it fell with a thud at my feet. I was genuinely impressed when Annie snatched it up from the straw-littered floor and deftly flipped it over Trigger's back. After tightening the girth and putting his bridle on, she led him out of the stall. She then gracefully swung up in the saddle and proceeded to the arena. I watched over the railing for a while, and then she stopped and asked if I wanted to ride. Although I was much smaller in stature than Annie, and Trigger stood way, way taller than me, I never hesitated. It wasn't because I was brave. It was because all caution had left me; I had entered an alternate universe, some mythic realm where heroines rode winged beasts with tails and manes flying in the wind.

I walked up beside Annie's winged beast, she gave me a leg up, and in a heartbeat I was sitting on top of the world. I have a vague memory that my feet didn't come close to touching the stirrups, but I held on to the saddle horn as best I could as Annie led me and Trigger around the ring.

Afterward, she handed me a carrot to give to him. Of course, I didn't know the proper etiquette or safety precautions regarding how to feed a treat to an eager horse. There is a trick to not getting your figures bitten, which I later learned. But it didn't matter. I was in love, and if Trigger wanted to bite my fingers to the nub, it was a small price to pay to be his willing slave. Lucky for me he was a kind and gentle soul without a mean bone in his body, and he carefully nibbled around my fingers as best he could.

That night I could barely sleep. I knew I would soon have a horse of my own, and the first order of business was to name him. I tried out hundreds of names and finally settled on Firefly. Don't ask me why that name seemed most appropriate. Maybe it was because I knew horses had fire in their souls and could fly like the wind.

The next day I started my campaign. I asked Mother and Daddy to buy me a horse of my own. My utter and complete determination was not apparent to them. They gave me vague answers about how expensive that would be and asked if I wouldn't like a bowl of goldfish instead. Goldfish! What did that have to do with what I'd just discovered was my life's path?

Like a river not to be denied its flow to the sea, I knew my parents' rejection of my request was no more than a small boulder in the stream of my resolve. I started a direct mail blitz. I wrote to both sets of grandparents, the ones who lived part-time in Florida and part-time in Maine and the ones who lived in Alabama. For good measure I wrote to all my aunts and uncles as well. I also started to read in earnest. I discovered Marguerite Henry's books *Misty of Chincoteague* and *Sea Star,* as well as the *Black Stallion* series by Walter Farley. Up until then reading had been a struggle for me. Now I was flying through books, hardly closing the back cover of one before opening the front cover of the next.

That Christmas I traveled with my parents, two brothers, and one sister from our home in Chicago to Alabama, where Grandmother and Papa lived in a magnificent Victorian house on a hill not far from the center of town. Not only could our family fit comfortably in their spacious home, our cousins could also join us for these noisy and festive occasions. When Christmas Eve finally arrived, I could barely sleep for all my excitement. I was utterly confident that, as sure as dawn arrives every morning, tomorrow would be the day my horse would appear. Every cell in my body vibrated with the knowledge that the new day would unite me with my four-legged dream come true.

The conviction I had about getting a horse that Christmas would have warmed the hearts of authors of recent books like *The Secret* and the myriad life coaches doling out advice on how the law of attraction works. To attract our heartfelt desires, they tell us, we must be like a magnet and align our thoughts, feelings, and actions to that single ambition. But for me there was no carefully crafted technique or intellectual process involved. It was natural and straightforward. My whole being resonated with the certainty that the following morning my horse would show up. Anything less than that was simply not a possibility.

When dawn broke at last, and I began to hear signs of life downstairs, I leaped out of bed with unquestioning faith that I would soon greet my new beloved. In no time my brothers, sister, and cousins were gathered around the tree, tearing into their presents. Without practicality to cloud my child's mind, I actually expected to find my horse under the tree. As the stack of presents started to dwindle and my horse was not among them, I became disoriented. I told myself that, of course, I hadn't *really* expected a horse to be here in the living room. He wouldn't be housetrained, after all. But surely there must be a toy horse, or a photo, I thought, some facsimile to let me know the living, breathing creature was close by.

And then, to my horror and disbelief, we were being asked to come to breakfast. I had not yet been presented with my horse.

I was dizzy. I thought I was going to faint. I became confused. It was more than disappointing—it was an existential crisis. When I look back to that time now, I can use words to describe it. However, my young self had no words, only the feeling of energy rushing out of my body, leaving me listless and drained.

As we made our way to the breakfast room, everyone else was giddy about their Christmas presents. No one seemed to notice I was suffocating in bewilderment. Jeff was thrilled with his BB gun. Butchie, who was younger, got a rifle that popped out ping-pong balls. Juliette cooed over some jewelry or sweaters or something equally dull to me. I had nothing to smile about. For me the world was gloomy, dark, and cheerless.

At some point in the middle of that most dreary of meals, Papa turned to me and said, "Justine, what are you going to do with your new horse?"

Did I hear him correctly? Did he just say "new horse"? Suddenly the gray fog parted to reveal rainbows and sunshine. In a fraction of a second I went from deepest despair to boundless joy. I couldn't get up from the table fast enough to run outside. The screen door slammed behind me as I rushed out to greet the most wondrous horse in the entire world. She was a young gray mare with a black mane and tail, and her name could only be Buttermilk.

The rest is history. It was painful to leave her in Alabama and go back to school up north. But I consoled myself by taking riding lessons, so that that I was a better rider when I got back down to my grandparents' house each summer. Less than three years after Buttermilk came into my life, my father and little brother died suddenly in an airplane accident. Still, my mother somehow made it possible for horses to remain a huge part of my life. It seemed she sensed the healing qualities these mythical beasts bring forth. I think her insight saved my life.

My dear grandfather heard my prayer, that long-ago Christmas, and made my dreams come true. It was a dream that was to last me a lifetime. Throughout the years I've enjoyed many horse companions. Some were high-stepping five-gaited saddlebreds, others were hunter-jumper types. I even bought a three-year-old thoroughbred off the track, and trained and showed him over fences with great success. But no horse thrilled me like that first gray mare, Buttermilk.

Being the third sibling of four, I often got lost in the shuffle. Juliette and Jeff got to name the games we'd play and, being older, they would always win. But when horses came into my life, for the first time I stood apart from my siblings. The love I felt for these great creatures, and knowing they loved me back, was something that was mine and mine alone.

Because of their strong and dynamic nature, horses met my fearless passion with a freedom and power of their own. As a young girl weighing barely over a hundred pounds and standing five foot two inches, domination of a half-ton horse standing more than five feet at the shoulder was out of the question. But no matter. The world over, we see a harmony between horses and women that defies the physics of size and strength. These sensitive animals respond most positively to the kind of interaction that comes naturally to women, that is, to befriend and cooperate. Like most horses, Buttermilk, too, had a natural willingness to befriend that made her uniquely qualified to cooperate with me. We spoke the same language.

Not too many years ago, I recognized that my granddaughter Meghan was also of the She Who Loves Horses tribe, and I had the privilege of helping to make her dreams come true. Seeing the light in her eyes when she climbs aboard her beloved Mountain Magic fills my heart with all the enchantment of that childhood Christmas when my own special dream came true.

In looking over the significant cycles of my life, I notice that horses have been my mythical companions, partnering with me to navigate the unfamiliar territory of grief, new relationships, personal growth, and much more. As I write this, I notice that I'm once more inviting horses into my life. I've made an appointment to take my first lesson in driving a horse and buggy. I wonder . . . what new cycle am I about to enter with these magical beauties?

THE WISE GOAT NAMED SADIE

Recently a dear friend shared this story with me:

> Tom had a prize-winning goat he called Sadie. Apparently she was a super milker. She gave the finest milk, in abundance. Another farmer got wind of this and asked Tom if he could borrow Sadie for a time. It was agreed that Sadie would make a guest appearance at the other dairy farm.
>
> Each day when the farmer finished milking Sadie he'd untie her so she could leave the barn and he would move to the next goat. But Sadie would stand inside the barn door and refuse to leave with the other goats. It was only with a great deal of cajoling,

pushing, and pulling that the farmer could get her out of the barn.

One day the farmer hired a temporary farmhand to come over and do the milking. The farmer asked the young man, "What is it with that goat?" Upon hearing the farmer's lament, the milker, who knew Sadie from when he worked with her at Tom's dairy, told the farmer that he knew how to get Sadie out of the barn. He demonstrated by kneeling down next to Sadie, putting his arms around her neck, and giving her a big kiss followed by the words, "Sadie, you did a terrific job." With that ritual completed, Sadie walked out the barn door with what I imagine was a smile on her face. The milker turned to the farmer and explained, "If you are going to borrow one of Tom's goats, you'll have to treat her the way Tom treats her."

I love this story. How wise that goat was. Giving milk may be strictly business to some, but to Sadie it was more; it involved a relationship of respect, cooperation, and even love between her and her human caregivers. She was like some grand dame who had a deep understanding that life is about more than the giving and taking of milk. It is about relationship, tenderness, appreciation, hugs and kisses, taking a moment to receive and give praise, and being told every day, "You did a terrific job."

When was the last time you complimented someone on doing a terrific job? When has someone said it to you? In our relationships with our colleagues at work, our family at home, and everyone else, let us remember to pause often in our daily dealings to tell each one, "You did a terrific job."

NIGHT AND DAY

S ome years ago I found myself lying under the vast star-filled California desert sky. I was enjoying the first dawn of a ten-day vision quest. The first blush of light was peeking over the eastern ridges. I was cuddled up in my sleeping bag on the floor of a very large arid bowl, its rim formed by mountains. To the east they are known as the Last Chance Mountains, and are part of the Inyo Range. I never did find out the name of those to the west, but I knew they blocked my view of the eastern slopes of the great Sierra range.

My sleep had been light. Often I would open my eyes and check the ever-changing sky. The progress of change was slow; if I slept for half an hour or so between glances, I wouldn't miss much of the show.

On one awakening I noticed the edge of dawn out of the corner of my eye, at about ten o'clock high in the eastern sky. Did I really see it, or was it my imagination? When I looked again with all my might, it had disappeared. Oh, it must have been my imagination. On the western horizon, night persisted, with myriad stars twinkling from a deep blue sky. But then I shifted my gaze back and forth, from east to west using a soft focus—Ah-ha! There it was again, the edge of dawn. This time I was sure I had seen it. I discovered that if I didn't look at it directly but looked in that direction without focusing my eyes, I definitely could see the edge of dawn. The dimmest stars there began to blend in with the emerging light, and soon only the brightest of planets still shone through.

My heart beat faster, as I felt like a voyeur looking in on someone else's intimacies—slightly embarrassed, but unable to look away. I was transfixed. There seemed to be a distinct dividing line between dawn and night, as if some light-filled dome were closing over the Earth. The dome kept obscuring more and more of the night sky until at last it reached the western horizon. Now the last vestiges of night were gone. There was no daily ritual to distract me from observing this transformation—no alarm clock about to go off, no morning paper to read, no phone calls to return—and I had the best seat in the house. Soon the sun came blasting over the eastern slopes, and I knew it would be a hot and dry desert day.

I wanted to observe this same phenomenon in reverse when evening came, so several nights later I settled into my sleeping bag sometime before dusk. I wanted to be sure I was early so I wouldn't miss any of the spectacle. As the light of day began to recede I used my shifting-the-eyes technique, this time looking for the dome of night. But it wasn't coming. In fact, the light seemed to put up a stubborn fight: It would not release so gracefully into night as the night had into day. I looked from horizon to horizon, east to west and back again. Surprisingly, there was a ring of light on the entire rim of the horizon. I could not even tell where on the horizon the sun had disappeared. And no stars were appearing in the east, as I expected.

Suddenly I saw a star, not on the horizon but straight above me. Now there were two, three, and more—and the brightness of the sky was giving way to a deepening blue turning to black. All this was taking place directly overhead. The light, in fortifying its hold on the day, put all of its energy on the horizons and left itself thin at the top of the dome. At last the day could hold out no longer and, opening up to the night sky with a great yawn, it fell back, yielding to the greater presence of night.

At that point I realized something that reversed all my former thinking about day and night, dawn and dusk, light and dark. Prior to that moment I had always thought of night as obscuring the day—a veil of night draping itself over the day, turning everything dark. Now I feel quite the opposite: Night is always there, always surrounding us, like a mother's gentle arms. Day comes and goes for us, but the stars are always there no matter what is going on in our earthly neighborhood. The veil is the light of day. Day veils the true sky.

Now when I look up at the light blue sky of day I feel comforted by the thought that beyond that brightness is the ever-constant, deep darkness of the sky filled with twinkling pinpoints of light—a place of exquisite beauty and depth that gives me a sense of profound peace, as I feel myself embraced in the arms of the universe.

OUR ANIMAL COMPANIONS

The lead article in a recent issue of *Parade Magazine*, which comes with the Sunday newspaper, was entitled

"How Much Do Animals Really Know?" I thought this synchronistic because I had just finished a book entitled *The Spiritual Life of Animals and Plants* by Laurie Conrad (Author House, 2002). So, animals and their interior lives were on my mind.

In the *Parade* article one of the questions was whether or not animals have empathy. Laurie Conrad makes a convincing case that animals indeed do care for one another and, even further, that they have a kind of spirituality. Conrad tells many miraculous stories about the animals she's known, from cats and dogs to wasps and mosquitoes. If you are an animal lover like I am, you'll appreciate the following story. Her cats Figaro and Alice had always had a difficult relationship. They were not the kind of friends that would curl up next to one another like we all hope for with our animal companions.

She writes, "This one particular night, Alice was ill. She was so sick that she huddled next to me on the rug. This was actually a very trusting and/or brave thing, because Figaro was in my lap above her and she was well within striking distance. Figaro was, in fact, ready to give her a good swipe—his eyes had that glassy, fixed look and he was switching his expressive tail. Alice perhaps trusted Providence and/or me to protect her, or she was too sick to notice.

"Seeing the inevitable outcome—yet also knowing the love Figaro's heart held, I appealed to his higher, more spiritual side. I inwardly told him that Alice wasn't feeling well and needed healing. I had to say this several times, and in several different ways. His tail stopped wagging and he began to relax, his body became its usual limp self and I could see he was listening to me. Then he did a surprising thing. He very slowly and carefully extended his left paw and gently put it on Alice's head. And kept it there, as though he were sending her healing by laying on hands, as I so often had done to him when he was injured or sick. His attention seemed clearly on what he was doing, and it truly appeared as though he was giving her all the Love and Healing he could muster. I was extremely pleased and proud of him, and I told him so, and he left his hand there for quite some time, until Alice felt better and walked away. Whether Figaro healed her, or my prayers healed her, or both, we'll never know. But Figaro gave Alice his Heart for those minutes, and in the end that is the essence of all Divine healing."

Biologist Rupert Sheldrake has graced our studios on many occasions. In one conversation he talked about challenging traditional scientific assumptions that pets do not warrant serious study. Well-known for his controversial and revolutionary theory of "morphic resonance" and "morphogenetic fields," Sheldrake applied this to the study of animals. He says that keeping dogs and cats is good for your health. Heart attack victims do better when they have a dog or cat, and older people have fewer physical complaints when they have animal companions in the house.

A friend told me a surprising story about her African Grey parrot. These birds are considered to be one of the most intelligent of all birds. She read an article about a woman whose African Grey would pull his feathers out whenever she had to go on a trip. Asking a vet about this, it was suggested that she show the bird a calendar before she left, pointing out each day she would be gone and then pointing out the day she would be returning. This seemed pretty far-fetched but since nothing else had worked, she thought to give it a try. Just before she left on her trip she brought a large wall calendar to her pet and pointed out each square that represented a day she would be gone. She then marked the day she would return and tacked up the calendar near her bird friend. Much to her surprise, when she returned the feathers were pristine and lovely. No plucking had occurred.

But, just to prove this was no fluke, one time she got caught in a snowstorm and was delayed in Chicago. By the time she got back, the plucking had once more resumed.

This story gave my friend Debra the idea to try it on her bird, Pico. She would always take Pico to a friend's house while she was traveling, but this time she added the calendar process. She didn't tell her friend about it. Upon her return to pick up the bird, her friend said, "You know Pico did the strangest thing this morning. He kept saying 'Where's Debra, where's Debra?' as if he knew you were coming back today."

I know these stories will remind you of many of your own. These loving companions enrich our lives beyond measure.

 ## HORSES AS TEACHERS

Through the years horses have been my teachers in life. The hours I spend on horseback dissolve into a timeless void as in sleep or meditation. There is no ticking of the clock, just fluid movement, single-minded focusing, two living forms becoming one as if in a dance.

I've often wondered why riding is primarily a woman's sport. Through many years of working in circle with women, I'm beginning to realize that women's power is the power to connect, rather than "hold power over" as is the case in a hierarchical social order. Horseback riding is a place where this gift for connecting shines. The best riders work in partnership with their horses. When this is done well, one can feel the horse striving to meet the rider in a celebratory equine dance.

One of my most treasured highs in riding is jumping over a course of fences. I'm constantly amazed at the willingness of horses to commit themselves to flying through the air with riders on their backs. Jumping combines in a practical way so many of the qualities I learn from my meditation practice: focus, balance, trust, letting go, being in the moment, and, greatest of all, unity with another living creature.

In nature what is the most beautiful is also the most effective and the most efficient. The same is true of riding a horse over fences. The perfect jump includes a minimum expense of energy for maximum effectiveness. One must be traveling at the right speed and take off at the right moment, all determined by the size of the fence, the terrain, and the stride and impulse of the horse. No two jumps are exactly alike. Even the same jump is different, depending on the mood of the horse, the weather, the time of day, and the attitude of the rider. When horse and rider are thinking and moving as one, making instantaneous judgments about all these factors, it's magic. When I experience a good jump it's like a *pas de deux* performed with perfect harmony.

Focusing is a priority in this sport. If my mind wanders, the horse knows. Equines are like Zen masters when it comes to reading your mind. They intuitively know that mind and body are connected. For example, if I approach a particular fence with fear, thinking we won't make it over, my horse senses my fear and will frequently put on the brakes just as we reach the obstacle—depositing me, *sans* horse, on the other side.

When I'm far away from the barn and my four-legged teachers, if I fall into a panic and my mind tells me, "Justine, you'll never accomplish this task; success will never be yours," I can bring up the memory of riding my horse and flying over a jump in perfect balance. Triggering this body feeling is like taking a magic "I can succeed" pill. I'm not pretending to be successful—I'm activating my body's memory of success. My mind does not know the difference between the actual event and the memory of the event. I can access my body's memory of success at any time and use the feeling of success to help me get through any challenge, in any aspect of my life.

When you find yourself feeling doubts about your ability to attain your goal, take a moment to remember a time when you, too, have enjoyed a great accomplishment. It is more effective if it is something that you accomplished not only mentally, but physically as well. The body has a phenomenal memory. In fact, some say it has a greater memory than the mind. When you're uncertain, let your mind take you back to your triumphant moment again, and feel it in your body with as much detail as you can. Recall the smells, colors, sounds, feelings, and surroundings. As you sink into this most pleasant memory, allow it to resonate in you once more as if it were happening for you in the present moment. Let the exhilaration of your success stay with you as you turn yet again to the task at hand. This meditation will be of enormous support for you in actualizing your goal.

IN THE EYE OF A WHALE

I n the spring of 2004, I gave myself the wondrous gift of five days with pods of mother and baby Gray Whales on the Pacific coast of Baja, Mexico. This experience has been life changing. Even my dreams are now watery and oceanic. In fact, I have made several return trips.

It was a "hands-on" event. Twice a day for four days, sixteen of us eased out into the lagoon in small skiffs, four or five to the boat accompanied by a naturalist or marine biologist and a boatman. We'd *putt-putt* to a designated place in San Ignacio Lagoon where curious youngsters and their mothers are known to approach boats carrying expectant humans like us. As we waited and watched, a few hundred yards away dozens and dozens of whales would breach, spout, and stick their heads up out of the water (we called that "spy-hopping"). Even if none came closer, just being in the proximity of four hundred whales was heart-thumping amazing.

San Ignacio Lagoon is a wildlife preserve, and only a few of the local Mexicans hold licenses to take people out to a very small part of the lagoon where "petting" is permitted. There are never more than ninety-six people in the lagoon at a time. The season is only three months long. Nothing like it occurs anywhere else on the planet.

We bunked on the beach at a place I'd call the Hilton of camping, powered by solar and wind. The food was an epicurean delight. We sampled many local dishes, including tasty local seafood. At the end of each day we would find ourselves gathered together, watching the sunset and laughing at the camp dog and cat chasing one another (the cat had the advantage) while we sipped margaritas. This slow way of living lent itself to the natural tendency humans have for storytelling. And how the stories poured out. We were living in what I would call our original nature, one of pleasant camaraderie, high fun, and creativity.

The setting was idyllic to be sure, but when we headed out into the lagoon for our first outing I was still skeptical. After all, these were wild whales living totally free. Why would one choose to approach us funny-looking bipeds in our rigid floating device? The thought of being able to touch a ninety-thousand-pound behemoth, or even her thirty-thousand-pound youngster, was beyond my comprehension. I told myself I'd be more than satisfied to just be in the lagoon with them.

My skepticism was totally blown when the first mother and baby chose to come up to us. First the baby stuck his head nearly into the boat, then the mother came to check us out. Looking into the eye of a mother whale who might be more than a hundred years old rearranged the cells in my body forever. This gentle presence has been on the planet for sixty million years. Humans are mere upstarts by comparison. We are pint-sized squeaky toys to them, reduced to yelps and squeals and one-syllable words like "wow," "oh my," and maybe an "awesome" thrown in. We sang to them, kissed them, laughed, and were silent in their immense and graceful presence. As they glided along on either side of the skiff, I imagined being accepted as one of their pod. Just knowing their large consciousness is willing to accept me in their world expanded mine.

Our hosts were Doug Thompson, Robin Kobaly, and Randy Davis of SummerTree Institute, along with author and naturalist Brenda Peterson. They teamed up with the Mexican crew of Baja Expeditions. The Mexicans were charming, quick to laugh and sing with us. They took good care of us on the water. We felt highly blessed to be invited into their dwelling place.

By the third day I was definitely in an altered state. Not since I was a toddler have I been in such uninterrupted, orgasmic ecstasy for so many days in a row. You might ask what that's like. It is a state of boundless, exuberant, and ecstatic awe. It was a true gift to my soul, one I will always carry with me.

Close your eyes and let yourself go back to a moment when you, too, felt delighted awe and boundless, exuberant ecstasy. It may be a childhood memory or a time with a lover or a friend. Let that time sweep into your mind and heart. Take fifteen minutes to write in your journal, and use this phrase to get you started: "Time disappeared and I was in a state of joy when . . ."

Let yourself write whatever flows onto the page. Don't think about it; let the words come spontaneously. Turn off your inner critic and let your heart move your pen across the page. Then take note of what you've written—and see if you can carry that sense of wonder and joy through the rest of your day.

LESSONS OF LUNA

We first interviewed Julia Butterfly Hill in October 1998. We talked via her cell phone as she sat high up in a thousand-year-old, two-hundred-foot-tall redwood tree she named Luna. Not long before, she had arrived in Northern California from her home in Texas, inspired by the efforts of a group of young tree-sitters to save the old-growth forests. Julia became a tree-sitter herself and climbed the ancient tree, knowing the loggers wouldn't cut it down as long as a human was perched in the branches. Nestled on a tiny platform anchored to the giant limbs, and supported by a team on the ground who sent the most basic supplies up via rope and pulley, the young woman initially expected to stand guard for a week or two. When we spoke, it was already a few months into what would become a 738-day vigil.

The conversation was deeply moving. Julia talked with us again from her treetop some months later, and we finally spoke face-to-face in our studio in Ukiah shortly after she descended from Luna. It seemed to us that with each conversation Julia was becoming wiser and wiser. I'm talking about the kind of sagacity one would find in a wisdom elder. Just twenty-five years old when she climbed back down to earth, she had become a wise woman in a young body. Michael said he felt as if he were sitting across from someone like the late spiritual teacher J. Krishnamurti, who lived to be ninety years old, or the late mythologist Joseph Campbell.

When we asked about her relationship with Luna, Julia said, "The only analogy I can use is one that people who have been married or partnered for a very long time might relate to—and I say, 'a long time,' because for two years I never left my partner. I needed her [Luna] to survive, and she needed me to survive. It was a true embodiment of a symbiotic relationship.

"Over the time I was there, she became the best friend I ever had. If I had a problem, I could pray and I would get an answer, oftentimes from her. Or if I was sad, I could climb into one of her many curving branches and nestle up and feel like I was being embraced. I didn't have humans to embrace when I was struggling. We often go to humans to help us get through in life. I went to this tree for help, day in and day out."

When I think of Julia in the tree, falling in love with her enormous, ancient partner, feeling protected and embraced, becoming wiser, I am reminded how innately we're drawn to the company of trees all through our lives. Children naturally go for what is healing and nurturing, and it is common for youngsters to build a tree house, or just to have a special tree to climb and befriend. I remember a special secret place I had as a child. It was a weeping willow tree that my best friend Marsha and I would climb to escape from the everyday world. It was secret and magical. The wind would move the branches and we would feel safe, hidden away within the tree's long tresses.

Julia Butterfly Hill not only climbed the tree, she lived in it, letting Luna's roots be her roots to Mother Earth. In the two years she lived in those branches she survived fear, loneliness, wild winter storms, and harassment from those who opposed her efforts to save the tree. But leaving Luna was one of the most difficult moments of the entire undertaking. "When it came time to leave," she says, "it was one of those things that still makes me cry, and probably always will. In the process I had become one with Luna. When it was time to leave, it was a ripping of myself, and I had to leave part of myself behind."

People often ask Julia if she misses Luna, or if she thinks Luna misses her. She told us, "When I looked down at the ground, knowing that I was getting ready to touch it for the first time in 738 days, I collapsed and began to cry, because I thought, *How am I going to be able to keep this incredible perspective I've gained, all these lessons I've learned? How am I going to be able to hold on to them when I'm on the ground again with everyone pulling me in a*

million different directions, and life trying to lure me away
from the invaluable, priceless gifts I learned in that experience?

"I prayed, and for the last time in her branches, Luna
spoke to me. She said, Julia, whenever you are feeling sad
or overwhelmed or frustrated or afraid, or feel like you're
losing the perspective, just touch your heart, because it's
there where I and this experience lie. That's where I will
always be, and that is a place that no one can ever take
away from you. And in thinking about it—well, I wonder
if Luna is missing me. I realize that as surely as I have a
part of Luna with me, in that tearing of the depths of my
being in my heart when I left that day, I left part of me
behind for her too, and we'll be partners forever."

What a privilege to sit across from such a warrior
woman, a woman who kept doing day by day what she
felt was right and good. Julia Butterfly Hill didn't go up
in the tree thinking that she'd be there more than two
years; she thought maybe it would be two weeks at the
most. But she gave herself over to her own life's right
action and was initiated like no other person I know of
on the planet. The body of wisdom and experience Julia
carries from living in Luna's branches is unique to her.
We are all the better for it.

TURN YOUR HORSE AROUND

It's been a while since I've spent an afternoon riding. Even so, I'll always feel close to horses. Through the years they've been some of my best teachers. When I'm on horseback I dissolve into a timeless void, as in sleep or meditation. There is no ticking of the clock, just fluid movement, single-minded focusing, a joining of two living creatures as if in a dance . . . becoming one. No longer two separate beings, together horse and rider become a new form. In that state, all kinds of lessons can emerge.

One of the best gifts I've received from an equine teacher is the reminder that when our instincts tell us there's danger ahead, chances are we can just alter our course a bit to stay out of harm's way. A feisty Arabian gelding named Morgan helped me realize that one brisk morning when I was walking him around the ring. It was cold enough to see our breath, and he was full of bounce. I knew he was looking for the first excuse to act out. From the corner of my eye I saw a squirrel scampering along the rail that surrounded the arena. Morgan had not yet seen him. My first impulse was to turn the horse around and walk the other way before he saw the bushy-tailed one. However, for some reason I did not act. I knew I was playing with fire. Part of me, I suppose, wanted the challenge, wanted the excitement; after all, I'd been riding most of my life and felt confident I could handle any outburst Morgan might offer. Predictably, when he finally saw the squirrel he took an enormous leap to the side. Despite my decades of horsemanship, I was almost tossed to the ground.

Once I regained my seat, I wondered why I hadn't followed my instincts and saved myself from a near fall. It would have been so simple. All I had to do was turn the horse around and walk the other way before he saw the squirrel, and I could have avoided the possibility of getting injured. I was shaken by the close call, and I began to think about other parts of my life where I walked right into danger when I could have walked the other way. I smiled and patted Morgan on his graceful neck to thank him for being such a good teacher. I resolved to pay attention to the times when my instincts warned me of trouble ahead—and to metaphorically turn my horse around.

Next time you feel you're about to be unseated, take a moment to find a way to turn your horse around. It doesn't mean you have to dismount; there's probably no need to end your ride. It just means you'll alter your course a little bit, then carry on and enjoy the journey. Chances are you'll arrive safely, with a smile still on your face, bushy-tailed squirrels notwithstanding.

SERENADE OF THE FLIES

O ne spring, my friend the late Sedonia Cahill invited me to join her on a vision quest she would be leading the following summer. It was pretty easy to say yes, because I knew that any adventure headed up by Sedonia was bound to be exciting. Besides, spending a couple of days in nature seemed like a good idea—some of my fondest memories are of camping in the mountains with friends and family—so at the very least the invitation held the potential of a very pleasant trip.

I got my first inkling that this trip was likely to be more than a holiday in the desert when Sedonia cautioned me that the quest would begin as soon as I accepted the invitation. She further reminded me that a decision to go on a vision quest is not something entered into lightly. She hinted that I might notice a shift in the content of my dreams and even of my waking thoughts as soon as I made the decision, and asked me to take particular notice of them during the months preceding the trip. She was prescient in her warning. Once I accepted her invitation, long buried emotions started creeping out from their dark corners and playing havoc with my mind. I began to ask myself, "What have I gotten myself into?"

It turned out to be an arduous seven-day quest. The first day was devoted to caravanning to the desert, the second day to setting up base camp. The third day we were acclimated to the actual quest and sent out to find our spots and establish a place where we would not see one another, and yet still be able to let our leaders know we were okay. The fourth, fifth, and sixth days were devoted to our solo time in the desert, with the instruction that during the last night we were to stay up all night praying and being receptive to receiving a vision in answer to our prayers.

We fasted for those three solitary days and were allowed only water to drink. Our equipment was the bare minimum: rattle, journal, pen, tarp, and a sleeping bag. The first morning I wondered with real concern what I could possibly do to entertain myself for the next seventy-two hours. I thought I might catch up on some long overdue sleep, but soon discovered that it was much too hot in the desert to enjoy a good snooze during the daylight hours. Sedonia had suggested that we pay close attention to any animals that might show up. I looked forward to spotting coyotes, but was more than a little apprehensive about running into rattlesnakes, tarantulas, and scorpions.

Much to my disappointment the first animals that showed up were flies—relentless, wicked, buzzing flies. There were at least a dozen of them circling my head doing their fly thing, making the most distracting sounds. I waved my hands, but that seemed to excite them even more, and their grating *whirr* went into overdrive. Nothing I did would discourage them or make them leave. I briefly considered getting under my tarp and just sweating it out for the duration of the quest.

I soon became convinced I would be driven completely mad by the end of the three days. My fellow questers would find me wandering around in the heat babbling to myself, "The buzzing, the buzzing." This definitely wasn't the Zen adventure I thought I'd signed up for. There was no place to hide, no screen door barrier to slam shut. I was in the flies' living room and they were determined to entertain me as their *honored* guest, no matter how insistent I was to the contrary. I was their captive audience, their revenge for every spider that trapped and devoured their cousins in her web. I was wrapped in a buzzing net of sound, and no amount of struggle was going to set me free.

Exhausted by it all, I finally resorted to my meditation practice. Sitting straight with my legs folded, hands resting relaxed on my knees, eyes partially closed, breathing easily in and out, I began to calm down. The cacophony of the flies began to calm down as well. It didn't go away, but either I started to get used to it or it actually became a mellower hum. Soon my aggravation was displaced by curiosity. Was I hearing individual flies? Were they buzzing on different notes? Were they making melodies, complete with harmonies? I imagined myself with a set of the finest Bose headphones over my ears as I began to hear a blended ensemble of the music of the flies. Like a mariachi band, they were serenading me.

Smiling, I realized these tiny beings were bringing me a gift. It was simply a matter of focus. I could continue my fruitless efforts at trying to control that which could not be controlled. Or I could relax, be curious, and stay open to a new experience. What had been intolerable only moments before became pleasant and enjoyable.

I enjoyed the serenade for a few minutes, then decided to take a walk. As I stood up, my tiny companions went into an ecstasy of excitement and burst into a jumble of jazz, and I laughed out loud as I imagined them acting like a bunch of excited puppies getting ready to go out for a walk. I even said out loud to them, "Yes, indeed, we're going for a walk." A short distance down the path they left and didn't return.

When we all gathered together at the end of our solitary days, the other questers reported being visited by all the animals I expected to see—coyotes, vultures, even a rattlesnake or two. No one reported on being visited by a flight of flies. It was my singular pleasure.

When we decide to take time out to listen and pay attention to what's most true and sacred in our lives, what shows up can be surprising. Even a "lowly" creature we rarely pay attention to, like a fly, can be a teacher.

Be an Activist without
Driving Yourself Crazy

TRIM TAB FACTOR:

TINY CHANGES THAT MAKE THE WORLD A BETTER PLACE

We live in a complex, adaptive system where everything is intricately interconnected. It is a multidimensional web of life. A small change in this vast web can, and does, affect the whole in ways we can only imagine.

The late anticipatory design scientist R. Buckminster Fuller often talked about the trim tab factor. To understand this phenomenon, imagine a large oceangoing ship. To turn this enormous vessel in a new direction, one must first adjust the trim tab, a miniscule rudder that runs the length of the larger rudder; once the trim tab is turned, the larger rudder follows. In fact, there are no mechanics yet devised that could turn the large rudder against the momentum of such a massive vessel without it breaking off. Only by first applying pressure to the trim tab will the larger rudder even begin to move, thereby changing the direction of the ship.

The world at large is a lot like that massive vessel, and sometimes it seems it's heading in all the wrong directions. Day after day we hear reports of systems breakdowns, social injustice, environmental disasters, weather changes, political chicanery, and more. It's tempting to pull the rhetorical covers over our heads and decide the problems are too enormous for us to believe we might make a difference for the better. But if we do that we take ourselves out of the game. We can no longer affect the whole; we withhold our wisdom, experience, and passionate enthusiasm, and our voices will not be heard in the circle of life.

Like you, I passionately want to make a difference toward a better life for all, and I see before me a vast horizon filled with a multitude of actions that beg for my attention. The changes that I see as necessary take on mythic proportions. So, to keep myself in the game I say to myself, "I don't have to do everything; however, I need to do something." Therefore, each and every day I do something. It might be an overt action, it might be taking good care of myself, or it might be having deep dialogues with others. I call my congressperson, I write a letter, I sign a petition. I educate myself, I have a conversation. I take a walk in nature, I lie in my hammock. I give thanks.

Gratitude is one trim tab factor on the small vessel that is my life. Melody Beattie, author of *52 Weeks of Conscious Contact: Meditations for Connecting with God, Self, and Others*, says, "Gratitude unlocks the fullness of life. It turns what we have into enough, and more. It turns denial into acceptance, chaos to order, confusion to clarity. It can turn a meal into a feast, a house into a home, a stranger into a friend. Gratitude makes sense of our past, brings peace for today, and creates a vision for tomorrow." I can walk another mile when I'm grateful. I stay in the game; I'm a player on the field of life when I'm grateful. I walk with greater confidence, I have more optimism, and I live with greater health because gratitude actually affects my immune system by relaxing me physiologically and allowing more oxygen into my system.

All of these benefits give me more energy to act—and action is a trim tab factor on the world at large. Every time I do one small thing to make the world a better place, it's like adjusting the trim tab on the giant vessel of some pending—or actual—global disaster. My effort may seem small in comparison, but it is a necessary component in the grand scheme of things that ultimately turns the tide one direction or another.

I have a small altar on the dashboard of my car. Every day when I enter that sacred space I do a prayer of gratitude before I start the car. I say a prayer for those in need, I ask for blessings on my day, and I give gratitude for at least five blessings in my life. It may be for the bird song that I hear in that moment, or for the blooming roses in my garden, or for the colleagues walking this path with me. Or it may be for the little things each of us does each day to make the world a better place.

Ask yourself, "What little reminder can I set up for myself to help me express gratitude every day? What can I do to adjust the trim tab on my life?"

THE PURSUIT OF HAPPINESS

Several years ago Michael and I read a newspaper article about the Secret Society of Happy People. It turns out that the group's founder, Pamela Gail Johnson, had declared August 8, 1999, the first National Admit You're Happy Day. Johnson, the author of *Don't Even Think of Raining on My Parade,* requested proclamations from the governors of all fifty states, but as the news release pointed out, "to the surprise of the Society, it became obvious that even in the world of politics, the expression of happiness was a potentially controversial topic."

The Secret Society of Happy People was formed in August 1998 to encourage the expression of happiness and discourage raining on others' happiness parades. Clearly the organization has found its niche: More than two million people from around the world have visited the website since December 1998. (You can find it at www.sohp.com.)

By the summer of 1999, twenty governors had declared August 8 as Admit You're Happy Day. But it had been an uphill battle. The *San Jose Mercury News* quoted Ms. Johnson as saying that then Governor George Pataki of New York had responded through an aide in his office. "We have no official position on happiness," he said. "We're going to wait and see what the federal government and other governors do. We may not know until August 7." Oklahoma Governor Frank Keating's office commented, "We'll need to check with our attorneys." Minnesota Governor Jesse Ventura's office replied, "[Governor Ventura] represents the people of Minnesota and he really doesn't see how this impacts them." Governor Bill Owens of Colorado at first issued the proclamation and then rescinded it. When asked why, an aide replied, "I don't know. They didn't mean to send it."

Thank goodness we don't need any proclamations, and we don't need to ask our governors to declare that it is okay to feel happy and to express it to others. We only need to do it. So often we fail to let our happiness bubble out because we are afraid we might be disappointed, or it's not cool, or we're being naïve or shallow. But when people express happiness, it does not necessarily mean they are unaware of the many challenges and hardships that so many are facing on the planet. They may just be part of a wonderful grand scheme that keeps us all in eternal balance. After all, for every negative event taking place in the world there are millions of kindnesses going on—and someone, somewhere, is happy.

MAKING A POSITIVE
DIFFERENCE BY EMAIL

Every day I receive emailed reports from caring friends about the challenges we face as a global culture. Each of these emails is highly informative and points out that bad things can no longer happen behind closed doors. Through this electronic network, all of us are now privy to information about the many injustices and environmental challenges as they unfold. More than ever we are aware of the suffering of others across this globe.

For me, and I know for you, knowledge is not enough. We need to take some positive action. Otherwise we end up feeling numb and passive or, worse, we become depressed and immobile.

Many of us participate in the global education process by passing information along to our circle of contacts via email. One way to be even more effective—and to satisfy your need to take action—is to take a moment before you press the "Forward" button on your email toolbar to write a couple of personal lines about why this particular issue is important to you. Then think of some action related to the issue that you'd like your friends to take. If that includes writing or calling someone, search out the correct address, name, or phone number. This will ensure more people will stand up with you to make a louder noise. Remember the old adage, the "squeaky wheel gets the oil." The more noise we make—that is, the more action we take—the greater impact we will have. The easier we make it for each other to take an action, the better off we all will be.

A good example is an action taken by spiritual activist Marianne Williamson during the 2000 summer Olympics in Australia. Early in the games, an advertisement by Nike was aired that showed a masked man with a chainsaw chasing a woman through the woods. When Marianne saw the ad, she was so incensed that she wrote about it in an email and sent it to some of her friends. In that email she included the names, addresses, and phone numbers of the president and CEO of NBC and the president of Nike. That message subsequently got forwarded to hundreds and eventually thousands of others who responded with equal passion, and within twenty-four hours the ad was pulled by NBC. The effectiveness of the campaign was empowering and uplifting to all those who participated, and it sent a strong message to the networks that depicting such violence against women will not be tolerated.

I believe we need to complain and stand up and be counted for what we see that is unsustainable, inhumane, and shortsighted. It's equally important to celebrate what is healthy, courageous, and decent. We all want to make a difference in ways that can truly be of benefit to others and to life on this planet. With this in mind, I encourage you to do a little more research before you automatically forward an email. Find the name and address of a key contact person and include this information with the email. You might even include a sample letter you have written or describe another action you are taking. When we multiply this action by tens of millions of concerned people, the world will surely change for the better.

KEEPING HOPE ALIVE

If I were to pick an image that would symbolize the current times in which we live, it would be that of one great big head. We live in our heads, talk from our heads, move from our heads, and create from our heads. We spend so little time feeling the animal of our bodies and tapping into the profound wisdom it contains. Whatever activities we can find to balance this mental chatter will, no doubt, lead us to a more soulful life.

It is the mental arena that most takes us into fear of the future, worry, angst, and anxiety, and cuts us off from our own deep wisdom, optimism, and hope. Unitarian theologian Reinhold Niebuhr says, "We are saved by hope. Our salvation lies in our belief in the openness of the future." I love that phrase "the openness of the future." I know the future is open and yet in the dailiness of life I forget. I can get beaten down by the barrage of disasters in the world, whether they are natural or man-made. Even on a mundane level, the unending list of commitments I've made seems to slow me down to a crawl and I start to feel I cannot make the contribution I'd like to make in a small way, let alone on a larger scale.

How best may we stay in hope? Not, I believe, by thinking our way to it. Hope lives in the wisdom of our bodies: in our hearts, arms, legs, lungs, and feet. I believe it is important to ask ourselves what we can do today to grow our hope. Just as we care for our plants, watering and feeding them, it is important to water and feed our hope to keep it healthy. We can't *think* our way to hope, we have to *be* hope. So how do we *be hope?* One sure way is to get in touch with the ecstasy of the body, and there is a multitude of ways to do that: drumming, dancing, soaking in a fragrant bath, having good sex, eating nutritious food that's exquisitely and lovingly prepared, singing and playing music, and walking in nature, to name a few. Keeping the body happy is as important as feeding the mind.

The question I ask is, "What are you willing to commit to in order to keep yourself vibrantly hopeful?"

Hope, in Spite
of the Evidence

Recently I received a letter from a man who is grappling with the many injustices in the world both now and throughout history. He wrote, "When I read the goals of organizations like yours, I think how sincere and well intentioned they are—but also how naïve. The assumption is that the law of averages is miraculously going to overcome poverty and injustice, and that transformation will occur because it has to be so. I ask, why does it have to be so just because it seems right? Maybe there is a reason for the human tragedy that we have not thought of."

I was compelled to respond. I found myself writing about some of the things that inspire me to get up every morning, and to do the work that gives my life meaning. Here is what I told him:

I am inspired by the persistence of growing green things. For example, a single blade of grass can push itself up through a large cement slab. That blade of grass, once through, is joined by others until the grass itself is starting to make rubble out of the cement.

I feel I'm one of those blades of grass, and that through actions—motivated by love rather than fear—I can make a difference within my sphere of influence. Knowing that a blade of grass persists against the seemingly huge obstacle of cement keeps me going in the face of overwhelming evidence that the world is in terrible shape.

When I hear about the devastation going on in the oceans, I produce a program about it with someone who is having a positive impact on the situation. When I feel the Christian tradition as spoken by Jesus has been hijacked by shrieking radical Christians, I produce a program with an evangelical minister who speaks from a voice of reason and love.

I can remember that back in the early 1970s the birthing process was treated like some medical emergency in a surgical amphitheater with bright lights, a drugged mother who was helpless to participate, and a baby pulled from her body with forceps. I started producing programs on this subject with such luminaries as Dr. Frederick Leboyer, who advocated what he calls "birth without violence." Since that time practically every hospital in the United States has set up a birthing center where natural childbirth is supported by a midwife, low lights, and a supportive team.

Also in the early 1970s, New Dimensions was producing programs on alternative and complementary medicine. The mainstream media laughed at us, but now it is acknowledged that more money is spent on this kind of medicine than on allopathic medicine. Insurance companies now pay for some of these alternatives.

I could go on with other examples of the changing of an age. New Dimensions has done programs on prison reform, peace, the media, work and livelihood, business, politics, and many other subjects. We are not covering all that needs to be covered, but we are doing our part. And that is the point for me. It is good to look at the history from where we've come and be aware of the terrible injustices that continue to emerge in the world today. However, we must keep doing what we can to change that.

As Michael Toms is fond of saying, "Hope is believing, in spite of the evidence—and working actively to change the evidence."

SERVING LIFE

We were born to both savor and serve life. These two qualities of being can be equated to our breathing in and breathing out. To have one without the other is to face collapse.

To savor life is to breathe it in, to enjoy its aroma and its essence fully. Close your eyes and take a deep breath right now as you let a smile form on your lips. Ah . . .

Now release that breath, just as you release your loving energy in service to the world, serving what you care deeply about, serving what you value in life . . . serving what you love.

As we know, the clock is ticking on all the challenges we face on the planet today. The good news is that we have done our homework: We've learned to meditate, and learned about the body-mind connection so that we can act from a place of strength and balance. We are now in instant contact over the Internet and understand that gathering the news of the planet cannot be done by sticking only to the six o'clock news or the local newspaper. We have learned to do research on the Web and to share that research with others. We've learned to probe deeply into what seems on the surface to be true. As elder Anne Dosher says, "In these chaotic times we must move from cognitive dissonance to inspirational dissonance by learning to live more deeply in the questions, and to ask new ones." No longer accepting the world at face value, we understand there is an invisible energy that connects us all to one another. When some catastrophic event occurs on the planet thousands of miles away, we realize it affects us. Dr. Martin Luther King Jr. spoke the truth when he said, "All life is interrelated. We are all caught in an inescapable network of mutuality, tied into a single garment of destiny. Whatever affects one directly, affects all indirectly."

We are living in the most extraordinary and exciting of times. We are the most informed citizenry of any in our history. And we are heartened by the words of Thomas Jefferson: "Whenever the people are well informed, they can be trusted with their own government; that whenever things get so far wrong as to attract their notice, they may be relied on to set them to rights." We are there now and are participants in this changing of an age. We were made for these times. The questions we are now asking are new, wide, and deep, like the question architect and visionary William McDonough asks: "How can we serve all the children of all species for all time?"

I know that many of us feel overwhelmed by the enormity of the change that we are being asked to serve. We see so much that demands our attention: the needs of women and children, the AIDS virus, wars, economic injustice, the spoiling of the environment, terrorism, corporations that are not accountable for the public good, and on and on.

I am often asked the question, "But what can I do?" My best advice is to look for something that is close to you that needs your help.

Let me tell you about a colleague of mine, Tom Greenaway. When he moved to Ukiah, California, to work in our offices here, he started attending the local weekly city council meetings. Every week he would sit in the same place. He never said anything, he just sat through the meetings. There would be times when hundreds of people would show up for a particular issue. The hall would be filled to its capacity, and as soon as that part of the agenda was concluded, the hall would be empty once more, with only Tom sitting there keeping watch. This went on for several years until Tom went into semiretirement from New Dimensions and moved to Tennessee. We had a going-away party for him, and someone from the city council came and said that Tom's presence, his nonjudgmental listening and witnessing, had made their decisions better. Because he was there, week after week, they held themselves more accountable to the public they served. This is a powerful statement of how our very presence can make a difference.

You don't have to do everything, but you need to do something on a regular basis. If you wonder what that might be, look around you. Inhale, and savor life. Check out what you are passionate about. Then exhale, and take action. You don't have to be assured of a particular outcome in order to participate. We can never really know what the results of our service will be. But whatever the outcome, do one small thing because it is the right and good thing for you to do. Do it because it makes *you* feel better. Do it with confidence and joy.

THE ABSOLUTE

AND THE RELATIVE

Early on in my relationship with Michael I worried a lot. Michael would help me stop my mind from spinning by asking me, "Justine, are you cold right now?" to which I'd answer no.

He would ask me, "Are you hungry?"

I'd say no.

He'd ask, "Is there a roof over your head right now?"

I'd have to admit there was indeed a roof protecting me from the heat and the cold and the rain.

Then he would say, "So, why are you worrying?"

And he would repeat the words of Swami Vivekananda, "What right do you have to bring worry into the world? To the extent that you are worrying, you don't believe in God."

That thought has always helped me to quiet my mind and take the next step along my path.

Later I learned something similar from the Tibetans. They talk about the "relative" and the "absolute." The relative is like the local weather with clouds obscuring the sky, making the day seem overcast, cold, and wet. But the clouds never touch the moon or the sun. They have no effect on them. The sun and moon keep on keeping on. They are akin to the absolute.

Now when I get worried and upset I know that I can choose to switch channels and move my consciousness from the local weather, or the relative difficulties of the world around me—which may not be too pretty in the moment—to the spacious bright sky of the absolute.

That doesn't mean I don't try to help modify the weather's effects for the better in the world we live in. It is important to do our best to comfort those who are cold, wet, and hungry. I hear some terrible tale of woe, and instead of allowing it to depress me or, worse still, paralyze me, I produce a program about it and do an interview with someone who lives in the field of possibilities. In a way, possibilities are like an energetic bridge between the troubled world of the relative and the bright clear world of the absolute.

Besides, living in the field of possibilities is much more fun than being pessimistic and cynical. Life is a joy, and celebration is always close at hand when we are working to change things for the better. It helps us stay in touch with the world of the absolute in a way that breaks up the clouds that threaten to darken the sky just above our heads.

Circles and Friendships

SITTING IN CIRCLE WITH

FRIENDS OF THE HEART

When I say I belong to several circles, people wonder what I'm talking about. Most everyone has a "circle" of friends. But I'm talking about something slightly more formal than an occasional get-together for coffee, dinner, or a movie. The kind of circle I'm referring to is more intentional, with unique qualities and principles that nurture its members to grow more fully into their fullness and beauty. As a result, they become more of who they truly are, with the confidence to take a stronger sense of self out to their families, to their workplaces, and into their communities.

One of my early circles was called the Spider Lodge. That name came to us after many meetings as this diverse group of women learned to weave together the multiple strands of who we were as individuals to form a cohesive whole. At the first meeting, sometime in the early 1980s, about a dozen of us consented to come together and spend a week on a houseboat on Lake Shasta in Northern California. There was no one in the group who knew everyone else, but each of us did know one or two others. Looking back on it, I'm amazed at our courage in entering an arena like that, one from which there was no escape. There was no phone (we didn't have cell phones back then) and no way of taking a break from one another except to just jump in the water to cool down when things got hot—and they did, not only because of the weather. Still, with sincere motivation, a great deal of trust, and perhaps a little naïveté, we all survived.

We had come together to explore how leadership could be shared, especially among women. Most of us had recently attended a women's conference and had come away feeling disillusioned by the way some of the female presenters had separated themselves from the attendees, as if they were somehow "more special." They did not take meals with the others, or mingle at social hours. They gave their talks and answered questions, but otherwise set themselves apart from the group with what we perceived as a rather aloof attitude.

On the houseboat we wanted to talk about this and see if we could identify the underlying malady. Most of us felt that what we'd experienced at the conference was the common order of conduct in a male-dominated culture where people are divided into categories and classes. According to that paradigm, in one category there are experts and leaders while learners and followers are in another. The truth is that each of us has some expertise to share; every one of us can learn from everyone else.

From its inception, the women of the Spider Lodge wanted to explore ways to meet that provided a safe container for each of us to practice sharing the fullness of who we were. We wanted to practice the kind of leadership that moved around the circle with grace and dignity.

So, for the next five years we met on a regular basis, most often for four or five days at a time, learning about how to meet as equals. We worked very hard to set out some principles that would help us understand more directly the power of sitting in a leaderless circle with the primary purpose of growing ourselves into better human beings.

One moment during that first gathering on the houseboat set the tone for this new way of being. We had already spent several hours trying to come to consensus on something. I remember that I was all in favor of finding a way to compromise. Previously this had been the "normal" way of being together. Each of us would accept getting a little less of what we wanted for the good of group, and we'd then be able to move on to other things. But on that morning, try as we might, we couldn't find a way to meet in the middle.

Finally, with some exasperation Robyn spoke up and said, "I'm not willing to give up how I want it. I want what I want, and I will not compromise."

I was shocked. This was not how I viewed "women's way." After all, we were the greatest of compromisers; it is how we've kept peace in our families and communities for centuries.

Robyn paused for a moment to let her words sink in, and then she added, "And I believe each one of us can have it exactly the way we want it as well."

What a concept!

Robyn challenged us to delve deeper and deeper until everyone was satisfied. Of course, this took longer. It was a more difficult path. We didn't have any models or guidelines to follow. But it opened up brand-new possibilities for the kind of egalitarian leadership we were seeking.

I learned so much from that beginning circle. One of the central hoops we had to jump through in the years we met together was how to feed ourselves. How would we accommodate the diversity of preferences, allergies, political views (meat versus no meat)? What time of day would we eat, would we all eat together, would we cook together? And much more. We made it through by grappling with all the issues, trying out many different solutions until we finally came up with one that brought us into communion. We realized that just having a vote would not work because someone would be outvoted, and that would leave us with winners and losers. In the end we each provided for our own meals, we cooked them (or precooked them) ourselves, and for the most part we all ate at the same time. We could choose to share anything with one another, but that was strictly voluntary. While we were sitting in circle (our formal time together), we decided that anyone could get up and fix something to eat, because some of us were hypo-glycemic and had health needs that we all agreed should take precedent over any formalities. The same principle applied to bathroom breaks. Anyone could leave the cir-cle to take care of bodily needs; if a person didn't want to miss anything, she could call for a break for everyone. All in all, we applied our strategy of meeting everyone's needs to our decision making at every level. As we reached beyond the patterns of leadership we'd all been accustomed to, our circle taught us new ways of working together that left us feeling both nurtured and empow-ered.

This early experience formed the foundation of every other circle of which I've been a part. I learned that if the intention of the circle is strong enough to hold differing opinions and views, and if the members are willing to grapple with diversity, the rewards will be immeasurable.

Another circle I've been meeting with for several decades is called the Owl-Eagle Lodge. It has become my primary women's circle. We spend our time together exploring issues in our personal lives and also in our lives as part of a larger community. As a reflection of this, we extend our collective energy outward in the form of various acts of service in our community. We've put together drumming circles that are open to the public in order to help others start their own circles, held public events on the subject of women and aging, and participated in theatrical performances as fundraisers for local women's shelters.

The Spider Lodge and the Owl-Eagle Lodge have been such a great source of enrichment that I now belong to several other circles as well. One of those is called Sheerdelight and has been meeting for more than twenty-five years. It is a mixed circle of men and women from a range of generations. Some of the current members had not even been born when the circle began. Now they are college graduates. In the early years we lived close to one another and met weekly. At one point we bought property together and lived communally for several years. Now we live farther apart; we stay in touch via an email list serve and come together for long weekends two or three times a year. We've seen each other through marriages, births, divorces, illnesses, career changes, world travel, and even the deaths of a few members of the circle. We've been through the peaks and valleys together and now sustain a collective strength for one another. Since each of us has, at some time or other, been "on the mat," so to speak, we can stand strong knowing there has always been resurrection from those hard places. We look across the circle and listen deeply to the pain as we each take our cosmic turns at despair and grief. Every one of us has learned through the consistency of the circle that we are not alone. We are there for one another with open hearts to bear witness to the joys and the sorrows that life brings.

These are the simple, but life-enhancing gifts that a circle has to offer.

A CIRCLE OF YOUR OWN:

TAKE THE FIRST STEPS

"Let us be companions in the quest that never ceases— the inquiry into who we are and why we are here. We remind each other of our inner truths and support each other in living our beauty. What a rare experience! To feel equally empowered to hold the circle, to question the process, to be held as vital and sacred by the others."

—From *Wisdom Circles*, by Charles Garfield,
Cindy Spring, and Sedonia Cahill

People are often amazed when I tell them I've been meeting in one circle with the same people for more than twenty-five years, and in another circle for more than twenty years. Invariably they are infected by my enthusiasm and are eager to hear stories of the many ways circling has supported and changed my life for the better. People who are new to this way of getting together are often inspired to start a circle of their own, but are bewildered by not knowing how to begin.

As with any other new venture, the first steps are the biggest steps—but in truth they are really baby steps. The key is to keep it simple, start small. Here are three initial steps you can take toward creating a deeply meaningful connection with others who will support you in your fullness for years to come.

Step One: Set Forth a Clear Intention

Years ago I learned from the Reverend Mary Manin Morrissey that everything is born twice. First it is born in the imagination, and then it is manifested in the physical world. A circle is no different. Set an intention to create your circle, and you will set in motion a chain of events that will make it a reality.

Intentions are most effective when they include as much detail as possible. However, in the beginning you will not know all the details about how your circle will evolve. Each one is different, and yours will be a creation of the combined wisdom and energies of its members. Just be very clear about your intention to meet regularly, and your expectation that those who join with you will grow into what I call "friends of the heart." It is important that you have a powerful expectation that your life will be well served when you meet regularly with others who are willing to be fully and authentically present. Most of all, don't be tentative in your conviction. Feel your intention as a firm commitment to follow through. Instead of thinking, "Having a circle in my life is a good idea," or, "Yes, I think I'll create a circle in my life," know in your heart that it will become a reality. Say to yourself, "It's as good as done. I'm going to make it so, no matter what."

Write your intention down. When you do, your idea will have form in the physical world, and that's the very first step toward the manifestation of your idea. You're on your way. Your intention might look something like this: "I feel myself sitting in circle with friends of the heart who, like myself, are committed to meeting regularly in a safe space where trust and caring are nurtured and where I can bring my dreams and my authentic self."

Step Two: Put Out the Call

After you have made the inner commitment, put up your sail and catch the wind: Tune in to other people who want to travel this breeze with you. You won't need a lot of people to get started. In fact, just one or two others will be fine. There is no magic and nothing complex about it. Begin by talking with a friend about your idea, and then talk to another. You may feel awkward at first, but be assured that there is a field of energy holding you. Human beings have been coming together in circles since the dawn of history.

If someone declines your invitation, do not be discouraged. Trust that the right combination of people will begin to show up. Remember, you only need one person besides yourself to make a circle. If two of you meet on a regular basis, using circle principles, making a sacred center (such as lighting a candle), speaking and listening from the heart, sharing leadership, speaking from experience rather than advising others, keeping the confidence of the circle, and making group decisions by consensus—you will attract others.

Step Three: Meet on a Consistent Basis

Write your circle time in your calendar as you would any important event. Make a commitment to yourself and keep it, just as you keep an appointment with your doctor. When someone wants to schedule time with you, and you look in your calendar and see that it will conflict with your circle time, say, "No, I'm sorry, I can't make it at that time."

There will be times when you feel too tired to go. Go anyway. Push through. Afterward, you'll be truly delighted you went. Meeting consistently builds a powerful and vitalizing bond and a strong field of energy. If your group is sporadic in its meeting time, this can begin to leak the good energy that has been built up. It is important to keep the dates you set up as a group and not let outside activities take precedence over your commitment to meet regularly. By treating this sacred time with respect, your group will build a strong container for the positive gifts that a circle can bring.

In the early stages of creating your circle, you'll find it helpful to explore the many books and other resources available to guide you. One of my favorites is the Millionth Circle Initiative. I'm one of the founding conveners of the organization, which is dedicated to sharing information and supporting the creation of circles in communities and organizations everywhere. Our website, www.MillionthCircle.org, explains:

> "The millionth circle" refers to the circle whose formation tips the scales and shifts planetary consciousness. The phrase comes from Jean Shinoda Bolen's book *The Millionth Circle: How to Change Ourselves and the World,* which in turn was inspired by "the hundredth monkey," the story that sustained anti-nuclear activists in the 1970–1980s to continue on when conventional wisdom said that nothing (certainly not ordinary people) could deter the nuclear arms race between the superpowers. A proliferation of circles with a spiritual center becomes a worldwide healing force by bringing feminine values of relationship, nurturing, and interdependency into a global culture in which hierarchy, conflict and competition, power over others and exploitation of the earth's resources are dominant values. Our aim is to celebrate the millionth circle as an idea whose time has come.

Following is an excerpt from the Millionth Circle Initiative website's guidelines for creating a circle of your own:

> Remember, each circle is unique and it will develop what works best for its members. These are suggestions and are not meant to be rigid and static.
>
> To participate in a circle, all you need is the desire, the willingness to attend the gatherings and to agree to follow circle principles. Each group determines their own guidelines. Here are some agreements that have helped circles to function more successfully for all participants:
>
> • *Create sacred space.* This includes physically preparing a space to accommodate the participants in a circle, usually with a centerpiece or altar.
>
> • *Listen with compassion and for wisdom.* This includes listening without an agenda, suspending judgment, being curious, and finding the underlying meaning in others'

statements. Also, it is listening for wisdom as it comes through each participant.

- *Speak from your heart and experience.* Speak one at a time. This includes saying what is true for you and speaking to the center of the circle, not to another individual. We offer our experience and feelings to the circle, not our advice. Also, we speak one at a time and invoke a talking piece when needed, to ensure that all are heard.

- *Invite silence and reflection when needed*, in you and in the circle. This includes listening to our own inner guidance before speaking. Also, we request silence and reflection in the circle when we feel it is needed.

- *Take responsibility for your experience* and your impact on the circle. This includes demonstrating self-respect and self-restraint. We self-monitor to ensure that our needs and expectations are being met. We ensure our contribution adds to the positive experience of all in the circle.

- *Keep the confidence of the circle.* This refers to our confidentiality agreements. What is spoken in the circle stays in the circle to help ensure a safe environment for sharing our experiences and feelings.

- *Make decisions, when needed, by consensus.* This refers to our decision-making process. Should a circle need to make a decision, it is generally desirable to come to a consensus.

With these guidelines and your good intentions you're well on your way to enjoying the gifts of joining with others in a circle. I encourage you to visit the Millionth Circle Initiative website for articles and resources including books, videos, and other groups that promote circles.

THE GENTLE TOUCH

OF THE BALINESE

U pon returning from a visit to Bali, I was filled with images of beauty, laughter, music, and dance. There were so many wonderful moments and so many beautiful places. But when people asked me about the trip, I found myself telling one particular story over and over again.

It was about our first evening on the island. Twenty-one people had accompanied Michael, Sedonia Cahill, Barton Stone, and me as guides and leaders of the trip. When we first arrived at Pertiwi Bungalows in Ubud in the highlands of Bali, our hosts met us with a grand greeting. The entire staff was present along with a delightful banner strung across the lobby welcoming us. After our eighteen-hour plane flight from Los Angeles, all of us were enormously grateful for this gracious reception. However, some of our party had had a difficult flight. Our friend Jaye was feeling quite ill with a migraine headache. I'm sure it had something to do with trying to squeeze her tall frame into an airplane seat only big enough for a munchkin. She needed to take her medication, but it was locked in her suitcase—and she had lost the keys.

I helped Jaye to her room, then decided we needed help from the innkeepers and headed back to the office. It was evening, and the winding paths were lit by softly glowing lamps. Even at that late hour I was cheered by the thick foliage splashed with brilliantly colored blossoms that bordered the walkway. I followed the path to the main pavilion and the front desk, where three Balinese men welcomed me with their warm smiles.

I determined which one spoke the best English and asked if they could break open a small suitcase lock. With an enthusiastic willingness to help, he said, "Of course." The youngest man went to get some tools, and the four of us marched back down the winding lane to Jaye's room. The men hummed a song as we walked.

We found Jaye lying in bed, obviously in pain. After greeting her, the men went right to work on the lock and had it opened in a jiffy. Then the eldest man, Artana, reached out, gently patted Jaye's knee, and asked in a sincere and concerned voice if there was anything he could get for her. I found myself deeply moved by his gesture.

As I walked back to my room, I reflected on what such a scene would have been like if it had taken place in the United States, in a Holiday Inn type of lodging. I believe it would go something like this: I would pick up a phone and call the front desk (there were no room phones in Bali) and ask for someone to come up and help open the suitcase. After a long while, most probably a man would arrive. He would enter the room and would likely keep his eyes down, careful not to look around the room. He'd know that someone was in bed not feeling well; one could feel it upon entering. He would not invade her privacy by acknowledging the person or the pain in any way. After he broke open the lock, I would thank him and give him some money as a tip, and he would leave. There would be no chance for any real human contact.

That small but meaningful event at the beginning of our trip gave me an immediate view into some of the differences between my culture and that of the Balinese people. Their orientation is toward community. In fact, I felt that we were invited into their circle from the moment we stepped on the property. These people had a genuine concern for our well-being that went beyond our status as paying guests. Their natural friendliness melted my tensions away. There was no hint of servitude in their demeanor; they radiated only self-esteem, warmth, and helpfulness.

Ah, welcome to Bali. And the rest of the trip lived up to that sweet beginning.

WOMEN'S WISDOM

I returned full of exhilaration from the Women and Power conference that took place at the Omega Institute in New York in the fall of 2005, where seven hundred women came together for four days. Among them were Nobel Peace Prize winner Wangari Maathai from Kenya; creator of the *Vagina Monologues* Eve Ensler; cofounder of the Omega Institute Elizabeth Lesser; Pumla Gobodo-Madikizela, a member of South Africa's Truth and Reconciliation Commission; Carol Gilligan, author of *In a Different Voice*; Jungian analyst, psychiatrist, and author of *Urgent Message from Mother* Jean Shinoda Bolen; actresses Jane Fonda and Sally Field; and many others. Although she was not able to participate in the full conference, author, poet, and actor Maya Angelou set the tone in the opening session with her regal presence and delightful humor. The Millionth Circle conveners, of which I am a member, offered a pre-conference workshop and also coordinated circle gatherings within the conference.

What was most impressive about this gathering was that, by design and also in spirit, we operated as one large circle—we were all leaders *and* we were all followers. At the beginning of each session, a runner would select a row at random and hand a microphone to the first person in that row. She would tell us her name and where she was from, then give a brief statement about why she was there and what issues were of greatest concern to her. She would then hand the microphone to the woman next to her and the pattern would continue until ten women had spoken. Each time, it became clear that all attendees—not just the speakers—brought great diversity and brilliance to the collective. Their contributions did not go to waste, as the workshop leaders drew from the insight of attendees and also from other speakers. In many conferences presenters fly in, give their presentations, then fly out. But in this gathering, speakers were also participants and stayed on for the entire conference. Many of them, in their own talks, referred to the wisdom of a prior speaker. It was a forum that allowed the conversation to build and deepen through the course of the week.

The most profound lesson for me came from a presentation by six women who for more than five years had been engaged in an ongoing dialogue about the abortion issue. Three of the women considered themselves pro-choice and three were pro-life. After all this time, none of the women had changed her mind as to where she stood on this issue. Some of us at first felt deeply disturbed—even despairing—that, after years of discourse, women of such intellect and character had all remained steadfast in their worldviews and their positions on abortion. Even so, the group had learned they could laugh, break bread, and support one another, even in their differences. They had learned to hold their differences in love. They had learned to "stay in community and keep talking." In the end I found that this gave me confidence for the future of our country. It helped me to see a ray of hope shining across our deep cultural divides.

It was no surprise to find countless nuggets of wisdom and inspiration to bring home. Here is one tidbit I got from Pumla Gobodo-Madikizela from South Africa:

- Nonviolence is always invitational. It does not lead to further shaming, which can be a slippery slope into more disengagement to moral humanity.

And from the dialogue on pro-choice and pro-life:

- You cannot erase all the obstacles and history that brought us to our differences. You sometimes have to put them aside in order to keep going down the river together.

- Hold the differences in love and stay in community.

- Keep talking, keep telling stories, the human stories.

- The voice of humanity is not a monolithic voice.

- Ask the question, "What would we have to give up in order to participate in the dialogue?"

- We might have to give up our ideas about people.

For four wonderful days we laughed, we cried, we danced and sang, we connected with one another and were touched by the deep wisdom contained within the group. We didn't get enough sleep, but left with feelings of fullness from drinking deeply at the well of women's wisdom.

WITH A LITTLE HELP

FROM MY FRIENDS

H ave you ever had the experience of feeling that everyone around you is falling apart, and you are the only one who has it together—only to find out that you've been stumbling around in the dark?

The recent death of a close friend took me on a journey of some surprising revelations about myself, and about how easily one can slip into a cloak of denial and self-righteousness. Like a fish unaware of the water she is swimming in, I was blind to the waters of grief and distress that were engulfing me.

My friend David Carter died a sudden death at the age of sixty-one doing what he loved to do, playing tennis. He was one of the conveners of a circle that Michael and I have been part of for almost three decades. Through our many years together the group has shared the full gamut of rites of passage: death, divorce, birth—the whole catastrophe, as Zorba would say.

David's was an especially hard death for me, not because I was feeling so much grief, but because I *wasn't* feeling it. I was going through my day with what I believed was equanimity, moving blithely above the fray, so to speak. I took note of other members of the group who, I thought, were wandering around in the confusion of high emotion. Proud of myself for the way I was handling the shocking news, I felt that my Buddhist practice was finally paying off; I was truly making progress on my spiritual path.

In truth, this was not the case. Living some distance from one another, I and several others in the group relied on the phone and emails to work out details of how to come together for a memorial service for our dear friend. As the days progressed my aloofness began to give way to aggravation with my friends. I felt misunderstood, or got offended just by their tone of voice. It got so bad that I began to want to withdraw from the group entirely. After all we'd been through in the past, I wondered, why were so many of *them* falling apart? I saw everyone else as the problem, the source of the difficulties—but not myself.

The evening before the service I became so estranged from several people that at one point I could not even imagine myself attending the event. I felt alienated and outside my circle. Still, although I had no idea how I could possibly get through it, I soon realized there was no question that I would indeed have to find a way.

Upon arriving at the service, I found myself in the arms of my dear circle mates who were emanating nothing but love and connection. How did it happen that I had been so blind to my own grief, and further that I would project it all onto my friends, causing no small amount of mischief and hurt?

As Stephen Levine says, "Grief has a quality of healing in it that is very deep because we are forced to a depth of emotion that is usually below the threshold of our awareness." My lesson in all this is a deeper understanding of the need to come together in mutual grief. None of us can ride above the waters of sorrow and pain alone. And the closer we can be to one another when our hearts are breaking, the better. Phones and emails are good, but they cannot replace the soothing and nurturing truth that we are physical beings with need for physical touch. Coming together is the most powerful way to go through such "depth of emotion."

Throughout the memorial I was surrounded by the loving presence of my friends. It was deeply healing to cry and laugh as, together, we remembered our dear friend.

CREATING A CIRCLE— ANYWHERE

Many years of sitting in circle have taught me to trust the excellence of this special way of being with others. What makes it work for me is the shape of the circle itself, along with a center that represents the sacred mystery of life, such as flowers or a candle. These two elements can bring the magical qualities of a circle to any situation—at work, meeting with friends, or in virtually any sort of gathering. There is no need to announce, "Now we are sitting in circle with a sacred center." We can quietly set the stage and let the magic happen.

In the fall of 2002, some colleagues set up a fundraising opportunity for New Dimensions, our nonprofit educational organization. They invited Michael and me to a conference center in the city to meet with several of their friends, all of whom were movers and shakers and highly respected in their various fields of endeavor. Each one represented a significant potential funding resource for our work. My anxiety and my hopes were high as we moved into the meeting.

When I walked into the small banquet room, I noticed there were no chairs in the room, only four tables. The largest table was in the center of the room. It was filled with hors d'oeuvres and several bottles of water and wine, and included a large, rather uninspired floral arrangement in the center. Three smaller tables were placed around the perimeter of the area, for guests to set drinks on as they milled about the room. The arrangement was designed for a stand-up cocktail party, so that people would feel free to mingle while having casual conversation.

I quickly realized this setup was not going to work for our purposes. Because of my experience with the power of the circle, I knew I could quickly reset the room to create a space that would better support deep listening and deep questioning. We didn't have much time before the guests arrived, but with the help of my colleagues we cleared the main table and placed all the food and beverages on the three smaller tables. We moved the large centerpiece to a table near the door. We then placed a simple candle in the center of the table just vacated by the flowers. To encourage our guests to flow naturally into circle, we brought in chairs and placed them around the large table, one chair for each participant.

We warmly greeted our guests as they arrived, and they soon began fixing plates of finger foods and helping themselves to wine or water. They milled about the room a bit, and then naturally gravitated to the table in the center of the room.

Once everyone was seated, I thanked them all for coming and also thanked those whose efforts had made the gathering possible. Silently, I prayed to all the invisible guides and helpers who I felt surrounded us. Since Michael and I were becoming newly acquainted with our guests, I suggested we go around the circle and introduce ourselves and the projects with which we were associated. This provided a check-in so that each voice had an opportunity to speak into the circle that we were creating together.

From that good beginning, the rest of our time together was extremely creative. Without drawing attention to the techniques themselves, we had applied some basic circle principles to support a dynamic field of listening and sharing. Lots of laughter followed, and authentic bonding and trust quickly developed. I'm convinced it was the power of the circle that allowed us to go so deep so quickly.

LOVE IN MY HEART:
THE STORY OF SHAW

At one point Michael and I belonged to a couples circle. We met for seven years with three other couples for day-long gatherings. Sometimes our meetings lasted an entire weekend. One of our members was a sensitive man named Shaw. He was an artist and had traveled the world. He had spent much time in India studying yoga and other spiritual practices.

During one of our gatherings we explored the ways each of us received and gave love. In a moment of profound vulnerability, Shaw shared with us that he had never felt love. He told us that he did not know how to either give love or receive it. It was something that was completely foreign to him. He didn't even know how to begin to join the rest of us in this exploration.

Prior to this, over the course of many of our gatherings, Shaw had revealed the story of his very brutal childhood. We all knew of the times when, as a very small boy, his father had ordered him to go down to the cellar and bring up coal for the fire. Shaw would have to battle enormous and very aggressive rats to do this. In a quiet and unemotional voice Shaw had described the rodents' shining eyes as they stared at him, challenging his entry into their domain. The image remains vivid in my mind even many years later. And this was only one of the many horrific tales he shared with us.

Michael and I had known Shaw longer than anyone in the circle, longer even than his wife. I knew without a doubt that he really believed he could not feel love. My heart went out to him, not in pity or disbelief, but with deep compassion toward a fellow traveler on the journey. I understood what he was saying, for I myself have had moments of feeling a great chasm between myself and what we glibly call love.

Some inner voice told me that I could be of help to Shaw in this moment. At first I doubted how I might be able to do so, but heeded the voice anyway. I'm so glad I did. When we help another, there is always the benefit of helping ourselves as well. I proceeded in what turned out to be a slow unfolding of events. I just kept trusting and following my inner instructions, which I truly believe came from Spirit.

First, I asked Shaw's permission to lead him in a little guided journey. Brave soul that he is, he said that would be okay. It is a painfully poignant moment when we are willing to give ourselves to others in the hopes of finding a deeper truth. We never know where these journeys will take us. It takes courage and deep trust.

I had Shaw lie on the floor. I wrapped him in a blanket and put pillows under his head and knees. I asked everyone to come around and put their hands on him in a soft, loving way. Then I took him on a journey.

I knew beyond a shadow of a doubt that Shaw was capable of great love. He clearly demonstrated it—both the receiving and the giving of it—in the way he lived his life. I instructed him to close his eyes and to let go of any worries, doubts, tensions, or concerns. When his breathing became easy and relaxed, I told him to imagine being in the home of his friends Carol and Steve. The couple has several children, and I knew that one of them, four-year-old Arisha, was a favorite of Shaw's. He was always talking about her. He would light up as he described to us her latest escapades, how she was growing, and just what a joy she was to him. It was obvious how much he loved and adored Arisha.

I asked Shaw to imagine being in Carol and Steve's living room and said, "Arisha has just walked into the room. See her smiling at you and running across the room to jump in your lap with her newest drawing." I then put my hand very, very lightly over his heart and asked, "What are you feeling right now, Shaw?"

In a quiet voice he said, "I feel a slight warmth in my heart."

I told him, "That is love."

We sat with Shaw, with soft music playing for what might have been twenty minutes or so. Then when he was ready, he opened his eyes. His entire body was expressing a big smile. He said, "Oh, is that what it feels like? I expected it to be big like a flashing neon billboard. This is small and tender, even a whisper."

It is easy to miss the whispers of love, especially in the midst of the harsh cacophony of life. Each of us has an Arisha in our life. It could be a child, an animal companion, a lover, or a parent. May we allow them to help us hear love's soft murmurings.

CULTIVATING ENLIGHTENMENT

I n the early 1970s, it was quite fashionable to be doing spiritual practices in hopes of becoming "enlightened." Even though it was said none of us would arrive at such a state in this lifetime, we were encouraged to give it our best shot. At the time it was quite a foreign concept for me, as I'd come from a strictly Christian background. But as I recall, I imagined enlightenment was a kind of destination. I hoped that if I worked with great diligence and dedication, one day I'd arrive there and forever after be in a state of constant, perfect peace and ultimate bliss.

In my life and work I've been exposed to hundreds of teachers, gurus, lamas, sheikhs, rabbis, ministers, philosophers—you name it—who have talked about enlightenment. Recently I asked spiritual teacher Arjuna Ardagh about it and he said, *"I'm not really a big believer in enlightenment. It feels to me that it is a term that people use very loosely, and no one seems to agree as to what it means. So, I'm not so sure there is one state that is universally referred to as enlightenment."*

Through the years I've made some peace with what enlightenment means to me. There may be those who have attained "Enlightenment," with a capital *E*—Buddha,

Jesus, Muhammad. For mere mortals like myself, enlightenment has a small *e*. It is a path rather than a destination. It is being in perfect rhythm with right action and right motivation. Although it is my highest aspiration to be in a constant state of flawless equanimity, I often find the best I can accomplish at this stage of my spiritual evolution is to *notice* that I've stepped off the path of calm composure before I stray *too far* into the morass of unconscious habits and reactions. I give myself pats on the back when I'm able catch myself and, with humor and lightness of heart, find my way back into the flow of loving-kindness and generosity. I like to think I'm moving in the right direction when I can step back into rhythm after falling off the path.

I'd like to share a story that will illustrate exactly what I mean. I've been interested in drumming and rhythm since I was a little girl and first played around on my older brother's drum set. Recently I attended a rhythm workshop led by the Austrian master percussionist Reinhard Flatischler. Some of the participants were accomplished musicians and percussionists, and some of us were total beginners. Rather than playing drums, we used our bodies as instruments. We learned to stamp out one rhythm with our feet, clap our hands in a second rhythm, and then join in with our voices in a third—all at the same time. We physically explored the layers of rhythm for as much as an hour or two at a time. It was an extraordinary nonlinear way of learning rhythms: Our minds were bypassed, and the information went directly into our bodies.

I never would have imagined I was capable of maintaining three different rhythms at the same time, and I suspect some of the others shared my skepticism when we began. But we had wonderful teachers. We all stood in a circle around Reinhard's partner and co-leader Cornelia Jecklin. She played a Brazilian surdo, a large drum that she had strapped on with a shoulder harness to ease the weight of it. Circling both of Cornelia's ankles were Indian bells that jingled when she stamped her feet in time with the pulse of her hands on the surdo. We followed her lead and used that rhythm to synchronize the movement of our feet as we stepped from side to side: right, left, right, left. We were keeping time with the universal beat, the one that never changes, the pulse that is constant around which all other rhythms are added.

Reinhard instructed us to start with the most basic beat. We marched in place: one, two, one, two. Then he had us clap a second beat: long-short-short, long-short-short. As we started to get used to stepping in a one-two rhythm while clapping in the one-two-three rhythm, he asked us to add a third rhythm with our voices using the syllables Ta-Ke-Ti-Na. It was a simplified version of what many Indian masters practice when perfecting tabla drumming. But for most of us it was not simple at all. We struggled to concentrate. We'd get our hands going and then our feet would fall out of rhythm. We'd get our feet going and then our tongues would get tangled in the syllables.

As we gamely tried to put it all together, Reinhard strolled around the inside of the circle playing a berimbau, which is a Brazilian instrument with African roots. It is a single-string bow with an attached metal resonator that amplifies the sound. Just to make things interesting, he was beating out yet a different rhythm altogether.

Once in a while I got all three rhythms going at once. It was ecstasy. I could hardly believe I could do it. Proudly, I thought, "Soon Reinhard will be opposite me and he'll hear how well I'm doing." But just as he arrived in front of me, I fell out of rhythm—I got all flustered and discombobulated. Reinhard burst into a hearty laugh, and I couldn't help but just laugh with him.

And that was the point. Keep it light, relaxed, go back to the basic beat and slowly add in the others. Have fun. Each time we stepped out of rhythm our teacher encouraged us to gently, and with humor, step back into rhythm.

By the end of the day it happened. There we were, maybe twenty-five of us, all swaying and clapping and singing intricate patterns that connected us in a single rhythmic community.

This is what enlightenment practice is for me. I know I will fall out of rhythm. My emotions will swell, negative thoughts will creep into my head. I will feel regret, and shame. I will lose confidence in myself and feel I'm not good enough, smart enough, or brave enough. The real work is to see how quickly I can recover and step back into rhythm.

Enlightenment is not far away and remote from our everyday lives. It is something that we can experience each and every day. We fall in and out of it over and over again. Remembering my experience of the Ta-Ke-Ti-Na workshop, each time I fall out of rhythm I remind myself to go back to the basic beat, the omnipresent beat that holds the entire universe in one inseparable whole, and step back into resonance with the rhythm of Divine Spirit.

A LOVING SPECIES

During the war in Iraq and the grass-roots struggle to end it, I opened my email each morning to find it bulging with writings on the political hot-box. Many contained stories that made me weep. Time and again I found myself wondering how our species could be so full of aggression and violence. Often I struggled to find a kernel of hope in the face of the burgeoning violence in so many places around the globe.

In the midst of this storm I opened a very special email that not only warmed my heart, but also rekindled my hope in humanity. It came with a photo attached, and the words, "This picture is from an article called 'The Rescuing Hug.'" The picture showed two infants lying on their stomachs in a bed together. One baby had her arm around her sister's shoulder. The article detailed the first week of life of the twins in the photo. Apparently, each child had been in a separate incubator, and one was not expected to live. A hospital nurse had prevailed over the hospital rules and put the babies together, in one incubator. Once they were together the healthier of the two threw an arm over her sister in an endearing embrace. The smaller baby's heart rate stabilized and her temperature rose to normal.

I immediately felt renewed with the deep, deep knowing that we *are* a loving species. Our natural state is a tender one. Helping one another is as innate as breathing. This drive to love, protect, and assist one another is programmed into our DNA.

When we become isolated in a culture of fear, our very heart rhythms are compromised. Never before in the history of the planet have we had the ability to reach out and be of help to so many others as we have now, whether in our own communities or across the world. The time is ripe to act on this inherent impulse. Let's fill the world with our loving acts—because that is who we are.

CELEBRATIONS AND RITUALS

LIFE IS FOR CELEBRATING

I am more and more convinced that life is meant to include lots of celebrations. When we fail to celebrate, we fail to notice our own lives. As I look at my own life I realize there are days on end when I don't make merry about the beauty and abundance that surround me. I can go for days and days being busy in my work, thinking about timelines, rushing from appointment to appointment, trying to keep up with my emails, my concerns, my political actions. Life can become overbearing with the business of solving problems and earning a living. As odd as it sounds, it seems much easier for me to put my nose to the grindstone than to celebrate.

My tendency to prioritize work over play became apparent to me recently when I attended a "Falling Awake" workshop led by Dave Ellis. I was shocked when he started the workshop with a celebration. I thought to myself, "This is going to be hard." Usually workshops put the celebration at the end, and I often wander off before the party starts, just so I don't have to participate in all that merrymaking. When Dave put such a priority on celebration, it made me stop and think. Later, when I came across that phrase "when we fail to celebrate, we fail to notice our own lives" in one of my old journals, the truth of it went straight to my heart.

There is no universal rule that tells us we have to wait until the end—of a workshop or a workday or a work year—to celebrate. We must choose celebration along the way. We don't have to wait for those special occasions such as birthdays, weddings, or that long-awaited promotion. Nina Wise, a performance artist and teacher, tells the story of a time in a hotel room in India when she was feeling very lonely and isolated. Immersed in her sadness, suddenly she heard voices singing just outside her room. She looked out her window and saw that the happy sounds were coming from some people who were living on the streets, who had very little in terms of material wealth. But there they were, celebrating the joy of one another's company.

I suggest you take a piece of paper and write down these words: "What I love in my life is _____." Take fifteen minutes and let yourself write whatever comes to mind. Don't think about it; just let the words flow onto the page. This is a truly wonderful exercise to do with a circle of friends. After you write, read your list aloud to the circle or to a friend. I know you'll be amazed at what comes to you. I'm sure it will lead to more fun in your life.

TIME TO PLAY

M y women's circle is celebrating its twentieth anniversary. At our last gathering we brought photos and articles to update the journal that we've been putting together. Amazed by the number of activities we've enjoyed over the years, we let ourselves fall into reverie over some of the more spectacular events.

I remembered one special time when Leah said, "My daughter is considering getting married." I was struck by her words, because it meant almost two decades had passed since this circle was formed and Leah was pregnant with Shayla. Beginning with a ceremony to honor her birth, it has been Shayla's coming of age rituals that have marked the passage of time for this powerful circle.

First there was a blessing way to welcome Shay to our world. When she came into her menses, she requested a ritual from this group, her mother's circle, but adamantly insisted there be no "New Age stuff." The young woman didn't want to be embarrassed by anything too foreign for her practical and down-to-earth sensibilities. She brought a friend to the circle, and each of us spoke the history of our own coming of age with deep truth-telling. We showered her with gifts as well. When she was grappling with the adult issue of getting married, Shayla came to her mother's circle once more, where both mother and daughter trusted the wisdom, support, and nonjudgmental field that this gathering had created through the years. It is deeply moving to me that this circle of women, through persistent attention, has truly established a bond that can be trusted by a young girl, turning woman.

There have been many other powerful occasions we've shared in these twenty years. We were the first nonprofessional group to perform the *Vagina Monologues* and went on to present about eight performances over a span of several years. The last production filled a 1,500-seat auditorium. We've called together drumming circles to seed other circles and put together events to deepen the dialogue about menopause.

But there is one particular occasion I remember with the biggest smile. It was an event that required only that we play. We decided to spend an entire day in San Francisco doing nothing but activities that titillate the senses. We planned to spend the entire day devoted to just having fun. We would take on the cloaks of women of mystery, dressing up all in black, including hats. Our chariot was a long black limousine driven by a gregarious man who really got into the "play" with us.

First we went to the Palace of the Legion of Honor and wandered the halls of its art gallery. We went shopping (of course!) at a clothing outlet. It is such a riot to shop with girlfriends, each of us ooh-ing and ah-ing over each other's outfits. We enjoyed a group tarot reading in a blossoming tea garden and walked the outdoor labyrinth in the moonlight at Grace Cathedral. All of us were glowing from the laughter and excitement of a day spent in total frivolity—no working, no saving the world, no planning large drumming circles. It was one blissful day dedicated solely to enjoying each other's company.

We knew there were people around us who were curious, for we were like schoolgirls just let out of class but encased in older women's bodies. At dinner the waiter commented, "Others are wondering who you are." Sedonia, with her peppered gray hair and exotic good looks, glanced up at him and without missing a beat said, "Oh really?" and with a flip of her head turned her attention back to the table and our group. We remained mysterious, even as we were whisked away in our black limousine.

The magic of that day sprang from the joy and spontaneity of a few hours devoted to nothing but play. It was healing. It was rejuvenating. And many years later it still stands out against the many memorable events shared by our circle. But sadly, for many of us, taking time to play has slid much too far down on our list of priorities. Maybe it's time to change that.

I suggest you take a piece of paper and write down these words: "When I think about playing, I want to . . ." Take fifteen minutes and let yourself write whatever flows onto the page. Don't think about it, let the words come spontaneously. Turn off your inner critic and let your heart write. Then take note of what you've written—and go do it.

 ## BE YOUR OWN ORACLE

I have several decks of oracle cards I use on a regular basis to help me access my inner wisdom. I might draw three cards at the first of the month to help me focus on my mind, body, and spirit. I like the cross-cultural nature of the *Thoth* deck by Aleister Crowley, painted by Lady Frieda Harris. There is a lot of depth to the symbolism in those cards. I also enjoy the artwork and symbolism of the round *Motherpeace Tarot.* I love the round cards because I've experienced the gifts of the circle and believe in working with people in circles. This deck even comes in a small pocket size. Recently I discovered a marvelous new deck of cards, *Wisdom of the Crone.* But for the truly big turning points in my life, I use the I Ching, one of the most ancient of oracles.

At New Dimensions we begin each weekly staff meeting with each person drawing one or two cards from a selection of more than two dozen decks sitting in the middle of the table. We go around the circle, and each of us speaks about an idea the card inspired regarding something personal related to work.

At a recent staff meeting I kept drawing one card after another, because for some reason I was not connecting with any of them. This was highly unusual because most every time I call upon the synchronicity of the invisible world through the oracles, wisdom shows up for me. I'm typically very moved in some way or another by the card I draw. My frustration was showing as I laughingly said, "It ain't in the cards for me today!"

My colleagues spontaneously came up with a plan. They all agreed that I could make up my own card. They asked me, "If you drew a card, what would it say?"

I immediately accessed my inner knowing and responded, "It says, 'Focus with humor.'" These words just came out of my mouth without passing through my thinking mind. They came right from my heart and my inner voice. I was surprised and sensed a wonderful affirmation that I knew exactly what I needed to do throughout the following week. I was gratified that my inner voice was so willing to share its wisdom. In fact, I felt that it had just been waiting, and seemed to say, "I thought you'd never ask."

I made a commitment to take time that week to be particularly focused, but not with the dogged determination that is accompanied by a tense jaw and squinty eyes. I resolved to do it in a relaxed manner, using humor and lightheartedness to lend joy to my overall mood, knowing it would then ripple out to the mood of the office.

Take a moment to access your inner voice. Close your eyes and take a deep breath. Hold that breath for a second or two, then release it with a sigh. Do this several times. Ask yourself the question, "What does my heart want to tell me right now?" Pause and let a few words float up from your heart. Try not to edit or judge them. Turn off your inner critic and let your heart write. Write down these words, and take ten or fifteen minutes to expand on what your heart has told you. Then spend a few more minutes reflecting on what you've written. Pay special attention in the coming week to the ways listening deeply to your inner voice helps you.

FINDING MY RITUAL

It was on March 8, 2000, Ash Wednesday, that I found myself stumbling upon a worship service in a Catholic church in Taos, New Mexico. I was at the famous San Francisco de Asis Mission church, one of the best known, most photographed churches in all of New Mexico. The architecture is stunning, but the church retains an earthy loveliness with its large sand-colored adobe bell towers framed against the azure blue of the high-desert sky.

I was taking the obligatory "I was here" photos when I noticed a woman and a small girl walking between the two buttresses that reached out like welcoming arms on either side of the church's recessed entryway. My curiosity was aroused as they entered the beautifully proportioned, white double doors, and like Alice in Wonderland pursuing the white rabbit, I felt an urge to follow. Once inside I was startled to find the small church crowded wall to wall with worshippers. Parishioners were crowded into the pews, and standing in the back and on the sides and even down the middle aisle. I realized I was in the middle of the Lenten ceremony of smudging ashes on the forehead, which for some Christians signifies the beginning of penance and fasting in remembrance of Christ and his sacrifice.

A kind soul made room for me in the back pew, and soon I blended in with all the other attendees enjoying the innocent voices of a children's choir. As my gaze wandered around the inside of this modest place of worship, taking in the various statues and icons, a deep sense of sacred presence swept over me. I am not Catholic and didn't feel I could fully participate by going to the altar to be smudged with ashes by the priest. But I did feel the sanctity of the ritual.

When the service was over, I felt inspired to take my drum and rattle and drive to the Rio Grande Gorge some twenty or so miles north of Taos, where the canyon is more than 650 feet deep. With reverence for the sanctity of nature's own church, I performed my own smudging with ashes, and beat my drum as I sent out a prayer for all the animals and plants and all livingness on this special jewel of a planet. As the drumbeats echoed through the canyon I could feel my life moving up a spiral. The ritual I had experienced in the church just hours before inspired me to perform my own ceremony, surrounded by the life energy of the Earth and all her creatures. I felt great peace as my spirit united with divine presence and all that is sacred to me.

You, too, can create your own ritual by going to your local river . . . or mountain . . . or forest . . . or chapel . . . or temple . . . or mosque. Let the spirit of all you hold sacred speak to you in whatever way you hear it best, and light the fire of gratitude and wonder in your heart.

THE NINE-DAY CLUTTER-
CLEARING FENG SHUI PRACTICE

There are moments at work when my mind seems to quit functioning. It's overloaded. It goes on strike. It just shuts down. I know this is happening when I start to forget appointments and can't find my "to do" list or my "needs follow-up" folder. I run from meeting to meeting with papers and pens flying, and I feel like the white rabbit in Disney's *Alice in Wonderland,* saying, "I'm late, I'm late, for a very important date. No time to say hello, goodbye. I'm late! I'm late! I'm late!"

When I finally notice I've spent another ten minutes looking for the file that was in my hand just a moment ago, I stop in my tracks, take a deep breath, and focus on my surroundings. That's when I realize I've been moving from one activity to another at warp speed, without taking time to clean up after myself. My desk is piled with projects, notes, folders, books, CDs, notebooks, flyers, dishes. The clutter is not only the product of my frenzied activity—it's a direct reflection of my state of mind. No wonder I'm feeling rushed, distracted, and overwhelmed.

I've saved a *Cathy* cartoon that describes me to a tee. Cathy is sitting at her desk, which looks something like mine, and she's holding the phone, saying to herself,

"Return phone calls . . . No! First clean off desk, then find papers, then return phone calls . . . No! First reorganize file cabinets to make room, then clean desk, then find papers, then return calls . . . No! First order larger file cabinets, then reorganize, then clean, then find, then call . . ." In the final panel Cathy is running out of her office exclaiming, "Help! I can't get my brain out of reverse!"

When my "mess" starts to get the best of me, I'm reminded of a powerful feng shui cure. You commit to moving, giving away, or throwing away twenty-seven items every day for nine days in a row. Maintaining the practice over this period of time sets a rhythm that can take hold and become a lifelong pattern of letting go. It's a powerful process that assists in changing the energy in your life from stagnation to flow. It can be used for the practical benefit of cleaning up clutter, and also to invite more beneficial energy to cascade into your life. The trick is to do it for nine days in a row.

I'm in the middle of my nine days as I write this piece. I have launched this effort in times past, easily accomplishing five days—then the weekend arrives and my flow is disrupted as I get into a frenzy of laundry, gardening, and errands. Suddenly, on Sunday afternoon, as I'm looking through a drawer crammed full of hammers, nails, miscellaneous screws, wires, and metal things I can't even identify, I remember my nine-day feng shui commitment. *Sigh,* I must begin again. Oh well, that just gives me that many more days to release more "stuff" in my life. And that in itself is deeply satisfying.

THE INNER ARTIST

WANTS TO PLAY

Remember the song from *My Fair Lady?* "Words, words, words, I'm so sick of words! I get words all day long, first from him, now from you! Is that all you blighters can do?"

Lately that's how I've been feeling. Days are filled with language, utterances, verbal descriptions, philosophies, arguments, and dialogues. My heart is longing to express itself without words. My eyes are hungry for color, my hands tingling for texture, my ears tuning for trumpets. When did I outgrow finger paints? Is that a box of collage-destined magazines I hear banging around in the bottom of my closet, crying out to see the light of day? My scissors and glue are on a rampage to cut, fold, and stick. My drums are thrumming at night in my sleep, "Come play me, come play me . . . do-wop, do-wop, do de do-wop."

Creativity is not a spectator sport. One must dive in and dive in again. Participating in the arts is nutrition for the soul.

I was reminded of all this as I was going over my outline for a two-day workshop I was invited to give at the Women of Wisdom Conference in Seattle. As I sat down with my intention for this gathering, I found myself imagining a booklet I would give each participant at the beginning of the workshop. It would be full of color, with a graceful logo, and inviting for participants to write down "ah-ha's," ideas, commitments, longings, actions, and next steps.

My colleague Bec suggested I use colored paper for the different topics I'd be presenting. Picking out some graceful typeface and finding an appropriate logo from a public domain book of Japanese prints, I delighted myself with this divine process of making up an inspirational tool to go along with the workshop, a booklet that artistically reflected my intention for the two days. I included a few quotes from *True Work: Doing What You Love and Loving What You Do,* which Michael and I co-authored. A local print shop added the final touches with a clear plastic cover and spiral bindings. Voilà! A finished piece.

Another co-worker, Flora, brought me the printed booklets. Holding them in my hands was deeply satisfying, like seeing a lovely piece of art finished with just the right frame. Oh joy! This is such yummy fun.

Remember, we do not live by words alone. I encourage you to get out the crayons, colored pens, and pencils, doodle a bit, and let the doodles take you beyond time.

FLASH MOBS: THE JOY
OF ORGANIZED CHAOS

Information flows around me like a small tsunami. My desk is fairly toppling with stacks of books, press kits, reprints from websites and newsgroups, downloaded emails, CDs, and more. Some of it seems almost smug in its gloomy approach to events, a veritable venting of what is going wrong in the world, the latest news about how the world is going to hell in a handbasket. Okay, okay, so we need to stay informed about the most current and troubling news if we are to do our part to make things better. But some days I feel I might drown in the never-ending tide of bad news.

Michael and I often end our day by reading to one another from something that seemed to rise to the surface on the tide of information. In scanning the various media, what we are *truly* looking for are glimmers of light. They appear like bubbles floating on the waves of bad news produced by the mass media. Recently, while browsing the "Datebook" section of the *San Francisco Chronicle* newspaper, a spray of light sparkled right off of the page. It was an article about spontaneous gatherings called "flash mobs." Writer Neva Chonin described a bucolic Saturday afternoon in a small park in San Francisco. People walked their dogs, friends chatted, and others sunbathed, while still others sat around in sidewalk cafes enjoying coffee.

Chonin wrote, "Chaos erupts at exactly 2:07 p.m. Sunbathers suddenly leap to their feet and friends break formation. Strangers begin grabbing one another's hands and running toward a central point in the park." She explained how they formed circles and began a game of Duck-Duck-Goose. "For the next eight minutes, bystanders stare as more than 200 adults act like children, gasping and laughing and tagging one another with screams of 'Goose!'" According to Chonin, the cacophony dissipated as suddenly as the crowd had formed, as echoes of delight continued to permeate the park.

My spirit grew lighter as I read the story to Michael. I was heartened to feel the confirmation of something I had already intuited: Imagination is alive and well, and is out celebrating.

Apparently these spontaneous games and gatherings have emerged as something of a new cultural phenomenon. Flash mobs materialize at a moment's notice, drawing all kinds of people together for no other purpose than to delight, surprise, be creative, and have fun. They are self-organizing and grandly imaginative. Leander Kahney of *Wired News* describes flash mobs as "performance art projects involving large groups of people. Mobilized by email and text messages, a mob suddenly materializes in a public place, acts out according to some loose instructions, and then melts away as quickly as it formed." This is happening across the world—and I think it's extremely good news. Flash mobs are a testament to our capacity for communal joy. Joy is good for the immune system and it keeps us in the game of working for the betterment of all life on this precious planet.

I don't believe it is frivolous to burst out in celebration with others. Indeed, it is an antidote to pain, despair, and disillusionment. In short, celebration just might be the key to our survival.

So, go to your email list and create some royal rumpus, for goodness' sake.

Celebrate Fiercely

I keep revisiting a favorite memory; it is a touchstone for me. In fact, I've even mentioned it in my previous writings. The scene was a fine spring day, and Michael and I were standing with visionary architect Bill McDonough on his front porch. Recent rains combined with the bright sun made the entire scene sparkle like diamonds. A squirrel was running across the emerald lawn, and flowers—goldenrod, magenta, cornflower blue, indigo, and hot pink—were standing in a riot of hues. I'd have needed a super-de-dooper box of Crayolas to match the multitude of colors my eyes were striving to take in.

The three of us were talking about R. Buckminster Fuller, affectionately known as "Bucky." He was the inventor of the geodesic dome and coined the term *Spaceship Earth.* I remember he often corrected people when they were talking about going into space. He would say, "We aren't going into space, we are *in* space." Bucky would add the fact that the Earth is spinning at 1,040 miles per hour as we rip through space at 18.5 miles per second (about 66,660 miles per hour) in its orbit around the sun, and the Milky Way is barreling through space at 185 miles per second.

On that memorable afternoon, Michael quoted Bucky as saying, "Form follows function."

Bill caught his breath in a rather pregnant pause, and Michael and I could see the wheels turning in his brain. He finally said, "Form follows function; function follows evolution; and evolution follows celebration."

It was so obvious, right there before our eyes. Spring was having a splendiferous party and everyone was invited. Everywhere we looked our eyes feasted on dazzling beauty. It was obvious that life is all about celebration.

Bill went on to say, "It's not about survival of the fittest. It's about those who celebrate the most being the true evolutionary winners. Nature is all about fierce celebration."

RIBBONS AND LACE
IN THE RESTROOM

Michael and I and our two colleagues Rose Holland and Bec Kageyama were traveling from our office in Northern California to Ashland, Oregon. We had a week of activities planned, including a New Dimensions board of directors meeting, a "True Work" workshop, and a fundraising soiree. Instead of flying we decided to drive, which turned out to be an excellent decision. Visibility was so clear we could see Mount Shasta's snow-covered diamond-like brilliance rising above California's high plain from a hundred miles away.

We drove up the speedway known as Highway 5. This roadway is comparatively new as highways go, and runs from Southern California to Seattle. The ratio between cars and trucks seems to run about even. For every fifty cars speeding by there are at least fifty trucks, and all of them seem to be in a mad race to get there first—wherever "there" might be.

A couple of hours into our trip we took a rest stop. We found ourselves in Maxwell, California, one of hundreds of towns impacted by the completion of the Highway 5 bypass. We felt as though we'd driven into another era as we pumped our gas on a main street lined with the facades of century-old buildings. Although small, Maxwell seemed a happy and even thriving town, despite the bypass.

When our tank was full, we noticed a tiny eatery named Topsie's. We were glad to see a local place instead of the usual colony of McDonald's, Taco Bell, and Burger King. Breakfast was on our minds, and Topsie's seemed the perfect spot.

It was a clean and simple place with a few booths, some tables, and a U-shaped counter with stools around it. We settled down by a window draped in red calico curtains. There were five older gentlemen sitting at the counter. They seemed to know one another, from the sound of their banter both among themselves and with

Patsy, the lone waitress. I didn't listen closely, but it was
the same conversation that was happening simultaneously in restaurants everywhere—it was about the
weather. One very congenial man with a sun-beaten face
came by our table as he was leaving and graciously
offered us his paper, which he had finished reading. The
gesture warmed our hearts to this town and its neigh-
borly residents.

After breakfast I went to the restroom before we
headed back out into the fast lane. What a pleasant surprise! Instead of the usual simple but functional lavatory,
this one was decorated with charming knick-knacks. It
had a large mirrored chest of drawers, with dolls and doll
furniture lovingly assembled on top. There were dried
flower arrangements on the walls and a profusion of lace
and ribbons everywhere. I was moved by the unexpected
care and creativity someone had brought to the place.

When I returned to the table I mentioned it to Patsy,
who said the owner was responsible for the décor. She
then invited me to take a gander at the men's room,
assuring me it was unoccupied. I can't say I've been in
many men's restrooms, but undoubtedly this one was
unique. The walls were painted a dignified dark green
and festooned with mounted fish, duck decoys, a buck
head with a full rack of antlers, an old rifle, and other

sporting items. It reminded me of a country gentleman's study in an old English movie.

The pride, care, and creativity the owner gave these two rooms lifted my spirits. Our drive through California's rural small towns reminded us of the importance of expressing our creativity, witnessing natural beauty, slowing down, and the grace of being a good neighbor—even when one doesn't know a neighbor's name.

I invite you to take a slower road to somewhere, sometime soon.

 ## SAVORING LIFE IS

A BIOLOGICAL NECESSITY

L ook around your space, inside your room or beyond the window, and notice something beautiful. Or close your eyes and think of something wonderful happening in your life. Or recall someone to mind who is special to you. Take a moment to notice everything about it . . . or him . . . or her. Immerse yourself in the experience. Feel it, smell it, taste it. Delight in it.

Are you suddenly filled with expansive joy? Indulge in that appreciation and know that this feeling is available every moment of every day. It is always close at hand. Breathe in the delight and joy that are your birthright.

It's imperative that we give ourselves regular and frequent opportunities to savor life. A passage from Rebecca Wells's book *Divine Secrets of the Ya-Ya Sisterhood* takes me to a place where I remember to slow down for the precious moments life has to offer. Sidda, the young woman narrating the story, is looking at a picture of her mother and her mother's girlfriends when they were teenagers. The photo caught them lounging on a porch on a muggy summer afternoon. Sidda says, "I want to lay up like that, to float unstructured, without ambition or anxiety. I want to inhabit my life like a porch."

Wells goes on to write, "Sidda was tired of being vigilant, alert, sharp. She longed for porch friendship, for the sticky, hot sensation of familiar female legs thrown over hers in companionship. She pined for the *girlness* of it all, the unplanned, improvisational laziness. She wanted to soak the words 'time management' out of her lexicon. She wanted to hand over, to yield, to let herself float down into the uncharted beautiful fertile musky swamp of life, where creativity and eroticism and deep intelligence dwell."

When we remember to take time to give our heart-and-soul attention to those things that are true and real, to savor the things that fill our hearts with love and joy, we find the meaning and fullness that make us truly alive.

I got in touch with this truth on one of my trips to visit the Gray Whales in Ignacio Lagoon in Baja, Mexico. On the shore of this exquisite lagoon, we were surrounded by the sound of whales breathing in and out, water lapping on the shore, laughter, birdcalls, and people singing. No one was telling us to tone down our passion, joy, or delight. We all got more and more silly with each passing day. Soon we were breaking out into song at the drop of a hat. (I remembered songs I haven't sung in forty years.) Everyone's natural humor was awakened. We were funny.

Near the end of the trip we were presented with the stark reality of how the world puts pressure on us to live in less than our fullness. While we were enjoying our last lunch together a film crew showed up to shoot a piece about the whales. The chief producer seemed very uncomfortable with our exuberance and laughter. He had not been touched, as we had, by the magic of spending a week in total rapport with the natural world in all her unrestrained spontaneity. He used words like, "You'd better put a lid on it," and, "You need to calm down"— which only served to send us into more laughter and song.

Like the culture to which we would soon return, his message was "behave yourself," "don't get too excited," "play by the rules," "stay within the lines." Hearing the producer's admonitions in the context of Baja, the whales, and all that laughter, I understood that my "wild darling" was out of the bottle—and she'd never go back again.

You might say, "Yeah, but I can't go down to Baja, I can't go pet a whale. And I don't have a group of Ya-Ya sisters to lounge on a porch with me."

That may be so. But you can savor life right where you are. You can take time to feel the wind on your face . . . to listen to the birds around your home . . . to relish the kisses of a happy puppy. A short time ago my former colleague Bec Kageyama brought a dog into the family. What a difference Lilly—that's her name—has made for her entire household. Bec takes walks with her every day, breathing, being in nature, and seeing the world through Lilly's eyes, ears, and especially her nose. On occasion Bec brings her to work and takes five-minute breaks to take her out for a potty walk. It takes them both away from the phones and the computer, out into the day to enjoy the fullness of life that belongs to all of us.

Let us all shuck off our preoccupations and breathe in the day and all its gifts. Let us savor life.

WHEN LIFE REVERSES

I had planned an early morning flight from a small airport about an hour from home. I'd even searched out the most efficient and economical transportation from the airport in Los Angeles to my gathering site. I was excited to be able to fly down to Los Angeles, spend the day at the workshop, and then fly back home to be in my own bed that same night. So I set my alarm for 3:30 a.m. and was out the door by 4:30 a.m. in what I thought was plenty of time to make my flight.

As I drove through the predawn darkness, I listened to Eckhart Tolle reading from his book *The New Earth*. I parked my car and walked to the terminal feeling good about how well everything was going. But when I entered the terminal, I noticed there was no one behind the counter. "Hmm," I thought, "maybe I get my boarding pass at security." I took my place in line, removed my jacket and shoes, piled my purse and briefcase into the bins, then noticed that other travelers had boarding passes in hand. At the front of the line I showed the attendant my receipt for payment for my ticket. He was very nice, but said the receipt was not sufficient. I needed a boarding pass—no exceptions. I was stunned as I began to realize that I was not going to be able to board this flight. The next flight was in the afternoon and even if I were able to board that flight, it would arrive too late for me to attend the workshop.

My emotions began to swirl, and my mind was racing. *I wish I had printed out my boarding pass at home. I'm really stupid. How embarrassing. What will I say to Michael and the New Dimensions staff?* On and on my thoughts spun out of control as I returned to my car. As I pulled out of the parking lot, the CD player droned on, and Tolle was talking about being conscious of the space between thoughts, reminding me to bring myself into deep presence through deep breathing. I felt miles away from anything resembling "deep presence," but I knew I had nothing to lose. And there was a chance it would keep me from spiraling down into a boiling cauldron of negativity. I turned off the CD player and tried the breathing practice he had suggested.

I soon realized that deep breathing alone wouldn't be enough to stop the emotional plunge, so I started chanting a Tibetan mantra out loud. "Om, Ah, Hung, Vajra, Guru, Pema, Siddhi, Hung." In a few minutes I tapped into a morphic field of the millions of people who have been chanting the mantra for thousands of years. The spinning spiral in my mind and in my heart began to slow down.

I remembered hearing Tolle talk about a man who had something wonderful happen to him, and all his friends said, "Oh you are so fortunate." He said, "Maybe." Then something bad happened and his friends exclaimed, "Oh, how unfortunate for you." And he said, "Maybe." This goes on back and forth—good things, bad things, good things, bad things. Tolle uses this story to demonstrate the point of living in nonjudgment. An event is neither good nor bad; it just is what it is.

I stopped the car and pulled out my notebook to look up a phrase I'd written down just the day before while listening to Tolle. There it was: "I'm never upset for the reason I think." Taking these words to heart, I urged myself to go beneath my distress to a deeper place and into the source of the pain. As I travelled north on Highway 101, with a tinge of light brightening the landscape, I began to feel a deep, deep sadness. I allowed myself to experience the emotion and to notice it in every part of my body. It was as if I were a little girl once more, and feelings of abandonment and vulnerability washed over me. I was forlorn and forgotten. Tears were running down my cheeks as I felt those ancient and deeply buried emotions come to the surface.

As my life was swinging back and forth between good fortune and not so good fortune, I was, for a moment, able to just be in the present and feel it fully. A deep tenderness swept over me, and for the first time in many months I was connected with Spirit, a beingness alive in my body, in my solar plexus, and in my heart center. I felt the love that never abandons, that is with me always, even when I am too much in my "monkey mind" to feel it.

As the sun rose over the ridge and the beautiful Ukiah valley spread out before me, I was grateful for that moment that connected me with Source even as I guided my car up the freeway. As the light washed over the hills and the trees, I knew my connection had been there all along, but my consciousness had been asleep to it. It took this sudden and unexpected reversal of plans to wake me up, and to remind me that divine presence is always walking with me.

WINTER SOLSTICE GATHERING

Both the winter and summer solstices can be powerful times. Each in its own way signifies the extreme angle of the sun in relation to the Earth. The summer solstice marks the longest day of the year. In the Northern Hemisphere it's the day when the sun is at the northernmost angle in the sky. The winter solstice marks the longest night, when the sun hangs low in the southern sky. It also marks the time when the days begin to grow longer and we can look ahead to the coming of spring.

The winter solstice, on the brink of the returning of the light, is one of the most sacred days in all the year. Our human family has used this special time to gather together in prayer and celebration for millennia. We see testaments of these celebrations in ancient stone circles, Egyptian pyramids, Mayan ruins, cave and rock paintings, and other relics of our ancestors' desires to mark their relation to the returning of the sun.

I reside near a community of people who live close to the Earth and build their homes, their work, and their relationships around a reverence for the Earth's abundance and her rhythms. They call their community La Tierra. A celebration of the winter solstice is an important part of the La Tierra tradition and reflects the way they value the Earth and one another. Each year for the past twenty years they have opened their doors to the larger community to join with them in marking this "Turning of the Light." It is a special time for friends who haven't seen one another for a while to come together, share food, and, best of all, offer collective prayers for the future. The event is elegant, simple, and always a moving experience that cuts across every religious denomination.

I consider it one of my life's blessings to be able to participate in these gatherings. Every year, I find that the winter solstice celebration at La Tierra leaves me with a new reverence for the great power and wisdom of the Earth, and filled with gratitude for the beautiful people around me. As our lives become more and more complex, and time to visit with friends gets squeezed into micro-emails, these occasions become increasingly precious.

This year's celebration was no exception. About sixty of us arrived for the event with sweets, finger foods, and wine. All ages were represented, from teenagers to mothers and dads in their eighties. The people who live at La Tierra had set up a room in a small building they call "the barn." Along one wall was a long table where we deposited our dishes.

In the center of the room stood a round table with a large, unlit candle in the center and 108 small votive candles arranged like spokes on a wheel coming out of that center. The number 108 has spiritual significance in many traditions. The diameter of the sun is 108 times the diameter of the Earth (give or take a few miles). Nine planets travel through twelve constellations in a year; 9 times 12 equals 108. Applying the principles of numerology, adding the digits of 108 together you get 9, the number of completion.

There were folding chairs set up around the room for those who needed them; many of us just sat on the floor. We all milled about prior to the ceremony, catching up with friends we hadn't seen in years. When it seemed most everyone had arrived, someone brought out a drum, and we sang a few of our favorite circle songs such as "Earth My Body, Water My Blood, Air My Breath, Fire My Spirit" and "Everything She Touches Changes." Even those who didn't know the songs quickly caught on to the simple melodies and words. Soon the barn was filled with sixty-some voices sharing the refrains of peace and camaraderie.

The lights were then extinguished, and it was time to light the central candle. This moment represents the return of the light of the sun, and it's a great honor to be chosen to begin the ceremony this way. As we waited in total darkness, a woman selected by the people of La Tierra lit the central candle and uttered a prayer. She then invited everyone in the group to come up, individually or with family members, to light a votive from the flame of the central candle and share their prayers.

And so we did. Some of the prayers were very personal. A teenage girl prayed for a brother who was sick, another for a grandmother who had died. A gray-haired gentleman spoke of a personal illness, a young woman hoped to overcome financial setbacks. Others offered prayers of gratefulness for the many gifts they'd received throughout the year. There were prayers for a better world, prayers for peace, prayers for the Earth. All of them were exquisite, heartfelt, and perfect. All of us opened our hearts, knowing there was no wrong way to pray, then held all the prayers as if they were uttered by our own mouths. As each candle was lit and each prayer was witnessed, the room became brighter and brighter.

Soon, each person who wanted to had lit a candle and uttered a prayer. But there were still some votives unlit. In order to get all of them aglow, we were to come up in larger groups to pray either silently or simultaneously aloud until all the candles were lit. (It turned out that in years past when each of the 108 candles was lit individually, the ceremony became long and tedious. This innovation proved to be a good solution to keep things moving.) At last the barn was bathed in shimmering, joyous light, and we could feel ourselves connected with the larger mystery of the cold of winter giving way to the warmth of spring.

I believe that part of the reason this particular ceremony is so effective is that this community has been hosting this circle every year for almost twenty years. Some of the young people attending were babies when it began. As teenagers they'd come to this recent gathering not because their parents ordered it, but because they chose to be there; it mattered to them. They were drawn to the ceremony like a moth to a flame, because the La Tierra community has set a field of energy through the constancy of the gathering year after year. And it was apparent in the prayers of young and old alike that they understood how each person's hopes and dreams of a better world could be amplified by the power of that circle.

The ceremony we held that night is one you can use just as I've described it here, or adapt to your own needs and inspiration. It's such an easy format. Calling in the light and hearing one another's prayers cuts across all religions. Whether you are Christian, Buddhist, Muslim, Jewish, Pagan, Hindu, or atheist, there is meaning and beauty in acknowledging the changing of the light on the longest night of the year. If you don't have such a gathering in your community, please consider being the one to make it a tradition, starting this year. You'll bring light to many hearts on a long winter's night.

ACKNOWLEDGMENTS

I'd like to thank everyone who helped me to write and publish *Small Pleasures.*

Thank you to the excellent people at Hampton Roads Publishing for your dedication to the evolving human spirit, especially Jack Jennings, Sara Sgarlat, Greg Brandenburgh, Gina Del Priore, and Tania Seymour.

I want to thank my hardworking, dedicated colleagues and workplace friends at New Dimensions Media: Rose Holland, Chris Pugh, and Albert Casselhoff, and my former colleague and friend of the heart Bec Kageyama.

To the members of my mother circle who, together, provide a community that has nurtured me, grown me, and inspired me for over three decades: Jody Baxter, Cynthia Baxter (you always said yes to my requests), and Danu and Atea Baxter; Claudia L'Amoreaux; Zoe L'Amoreaux Mapes; Dan Mapes; Tami Wands Bainbridge; Emma Carter; Conrad, Margaret, Aran, and Ian Levasseur; Tanya Anguita; Susan Davis; and Nick Leonardi. We've been through it all together—birth, death, marriages, divorces, living on the land together, walking the water lines, chopping wood, and staying up all night and listening to the messages of the heart. You have been true witnesses and mirrors to the struggles and cycles of my adult life.

I thank my women's circle for your enthusiastic support: Suzette Burrous, Marisa Clark, Elizabeth Davis, Alexandra Hart, Leah Martino, and Linda Merryman.

For all the friends and family who encouraged me to tell the stories that were within me. You believed in me before I believed in myself: Diana Hart, Phil Catalfo, Abigail Johnston, and the late Sedonia Cahill.

Juliette Sauvage, my dear sister who commented on the manuscript and whose insights were essential in this process. You kept me on the track of my dream when life wanted to pull me away.

To my husband and partner in New Dimensions Media, Michael Toms, and my son Robert Welch and his wife Lisa. I'm deeply grateful for your love, support, and encouragement. I'm so very thankful to my eighty-seven-year-young aunt, Helene Parsons. You have always been the greatest fan of my writing and your razor-sharp ability as an editor has helped to clarify and enhance this book.

I feel gratitude to Jan Allegretti, my editor, for your willingness to read and reread every essay, catching my mixed metaphors and other inconsistencies. You helped me to stay true to the message of my stories. It is a much better book because of your input.

And I thank all the former guests and listeners of New Dimensions Radio. For thirty-five years you have been the cornerstone of my life and work. You constantly rekindle my optimism for a better future for all life on this jewel of a planet.

Hampton Roads Publishing Company

. . . for the evolving human spirit

Hampton Roads Publishing Company
publishes books on a variety of subjects,
including spirituality, health, and other
related topics.

For a copy of our latest trade catalog,
call toll-free, 800-766-8009,
or send your name and address to:

Hampton Roads Publishing Company, Inc.
1125 Stoney Ridge Road
Charlottesville, VA 22902
E-mail: hrpc@hrpub.com
Internet: www.hrpub.com